ZE

A

# ZEEBRUGGE

## A Hero's Story

Stephen Homewood
with
Stuart White

BLOOMSBURY

First published in Great Britain 1989

Bloomsbury Publishing, 2 Soho Square, London W1V 5DE

British Library Cataloguing in Publication Data
Homewood, Stephen
Zeebrugge my story
1. English Channel. Ferry services.
Passenger steam ships: Herald of Free
Enterprise. (Ship) sinking, 1987
I. White, Stuart
363.1'23'0916336

ISBN 0-7475-0385-0

Printed in Great Britain by
Richard Clay Ltd, Bungay, Suffolk

'The dead have not lived and died in vain. They have brought us together – we think better of our kind.'

Elbert Hubbard

On the evening of 6 March 1987, the cross-channel roll-on, roll-off ferry the *Herald of Free Enterprise* capsized off Zeebrugge with 600 people on board after its bow loading doors were left open and sea water rushed in. A total of 188 people, 38 of them crew, died in the tragedy.

Stephen Homewood, then 34 years old, a married man with a young son, was Assistant Purser on board the *Herald* when she capsized.

For his heroic actions in rescuing passengers that night he was awarded the Queen's Gallantry Medal and the Silver Life-Saving Medal of the Order of St John.

This is his story.

# Contents

*Contents*

# *List of Illustrations*

# *Foreword*

Since that awful night so many people have said to me, 'What was it like?' This book provides the answer to that question. And not only to the events on the *Herald*, but what led up to it, and what came after.

I lost many dear friends, and in the aftermath came close to serious illness because of the stress and psychological strain in dealing with the memories.

The ghosts are still with me, and I suppose some will go on haunting me until my dying day. I would like to think this book can be an act of exorcism, and at the same time a tribute to the bravery – especially of the crew – of so many that night.

Stephen Homewood,
Folkestone,
October 1988

TO MY FATHER, AND TO MY SON SIMON

# 1

## *Capsize!*

The pens and pencils rolled first. Next papers, books and wire trays, slid uncontrollably. Then clipboards came cascading, video-tapes crashed down, chairs fell. And then there were screams, awful screams that I shall never forget.

It had all started with a violent roll to port, but the ship had seemed to straighten. It was as though we had swerved to avoid a collision. Then it rolled back, and this time there was no stopping her from capsizing. People were crying out in sheer terror, and from that moment it seemed as though everything was happening in slow motion. I gripped on to a partition in the Information Office aboard the *Herald of Free Enterprise*.

Paul White, the Chief Cook, to whom I had been talking, shouted, 'Bloody Hell, Steve, it's going over.'

And she was. At that moment I swear that I felt something very strange and almost supernatural, a deathless motion in the ship. It was as though she was a giant, living thing, and at that precise moment, as she rolled, the life, or the soul, call it what you will, was leaving her.

All around me was horror. A woman in a wheelchair came sliding past my office where I clung desperately for support to the partition wall. She had an expression of sheer disbelief on her face. It said, 'This can't be happening to me, someone pinch me, it's a nightmare.' Later I was to see a body brought out of the *Herald*, which I am sure was hers.

I had a direct view of the bar, where seconds earlier men and women had been drinking cheerfully, some of them clearly a little tipsy. Now it was a scene of mayhem. Glasses and bottles were smashing, trays toppling, and men, women and children were grasping desperately for anything they could hang on to. They screamed in terror at the tops of their voices at this unbelievable, impossible thing that was happening. The ship's list steepened so that the angle of the deck became even more acute, and the other drinkers started to fall.

The ferry's lights were still on, and I could see people falling with such speed and force that when they hit the large reinforced glass porthole windows at the port side of the ship, they left smears of blood as, unconscious, they slid down the glass. I was reminded horribly of insects and the marks they make when they collide with a car windscreen.

Then sea water put out the ship lighting system and we were plunged into terrifying darkness. From the first lurch to port the whole thing had lasted less than a minute. My first instinctive thought was for my son Simon. I thought, 'I want to see Simon again. I haven't had time to enjoy him.'

I could hear sea water rushing in. The ship was sinking and I knew that I would almost certainly drown. I have always scoffed at the oft-repeated notion that a brush with death sends your life rushing before your eyes – but that is exactly what happened. It was like a colourful and vivid fast film – school, relationships, my marriage, the birth of my son – all of it was there, whizzing past my eyes. The things I had never said, and at this moment wished I had, to the people who mean most to me; it was too late now. How I wished I had just said, 'I love you,' straight out, to those that mattered most.

At this point the upright partition which I grasped was virtually horizontal, and I was lying across it. It saved my life, for without it I would have had nothing to hold on to, and would have fallen at least 15 feet to the far wall of my office, killing or seriously injuring myself.

The emergency lighting came on suddenly, and a little of that terrifying blackness receded, although it was like putting a 40-watt bulb into a room normally lit by a bulb of 240-watt. As my eyes adjusted I saw motionless bodies, and seconds later the cries re-started, cries of fear, emotion and shock. Minutes before there had been at least 50 people in my view, and now there were just handfuls, frantically clutching tables to keep themselves from falling. I heard someone shout 'Mum' and another voice cry 'Peter'. Abruptly the emergency lighting failed, throwing us back into that inky-blackness. I assumed we *must* be sinking. I could not know that by the only fortuitous event of that whole catastrophe, the *Herald* had at that moment rolled onto a sandbank. Had we not, it is my belief that everyone on the *Herald* would have perished that night. The ship would have turned completely upside down and everyone would have been drowned in the icy water, unable to escape from the tomb of the ship.

I knew it was imperative to claw my way out somehow and try to start rescue attempts. Paul White had managed to climb around to the wall of the purser's office, which was now virtually a flat deck. He pulled me up there to join him, and we crouched, holding on to each other's hands like a couple of frightened three-year-olds. We could hear murmurs and wails of shock and pain; people calling out for their loved ones. The darkness was so total that I could not see Paul's face even though our hands were linked together.

Out of the blue our hands parted. I turned a full 90 degrees, calling out 'Paul! Paul!' It seemed such a terrible thing at that moment to lose human contact in that nightmare of blackness. I could not find him, but he survived.

I knew I had to make my way along what had been previously a wall, and was now effectively a deck, towards an exit to the outer part of the ship, and the hull. On that route, I knew, were the doors to the ladies' toilet. If the door was open because of the capsize, now it would be like a deadly trap-door. Even though there is a partition just inside the door to prevent passers-by seeing in, even a fall of a few feet might injure or incapacitate me.

I started to make my way towards it, bumping into life-jackets that had spilled from a locker. Suddenly in the darkness a hand touched my face from above. I jumped with shock, but then reached up and held it. It was a soft, slim, delicate hand, almost certainly a woman's. And it was totally lifeless. I felt for any sign of life, but there was none. She had clearly died instantly. But I could not work out, nor can I to this day, how she came to be above me, or where her body had lodged.

I let the hand go. There might (I thought at that time) be only minutes before the ship sank. I could not understand why we had not turned turtle, and I could not understand *why* we had capsized at all. There had been no collision, no explosion, so what could have flipped us over so suddenly and violently?

The truth, as everyone now knows, was so simple, so blindingly obvious – and to me at that time so totally unthinkable and impossible – that it did not occur to me even for a split second.

I got on my hands and knees and crawled, feeling ahead like a blind man, still hearing the frightening sound of the rush of water into the ship. I felt space – this confirmed that the door to the ladies' loo *was* open, and my heart pounded. I found the raised ledge at the bottom of the door, common on ships. I used it now as a flat ledge and inched my way over it.

Ironically I had just been reading a book on the *Lusitania,* a liner sunk by German U-boats off Ireland in 1915. From it I had learned what turned out to be a vital psychological lesson. When a ship capsizes, what was safe becomes dangerous, and what was impossible, accessible. In other words an innocent passageway across a ship becomes a deadly shaft when that ship has heeled over. It sounds so obvious, but the mind has difficulty adjusting to the concept.

Thanks to that book I was aware of that danger from the beginning. I knew that between me and an exit door was a passageway that crossed the inner-deck. Now it would be a near-vertical drop of about 60 feet. If I fell unwarily into it, and if the drop did not kill me, I would surely drown in the icy water at the bottom.

I reached the passageway, feeling gingerly with hands until they found the yawning gap. Across it, in what was now an inverted stairwell, I could see lights beginning to flicker. They were the collected tiny flames of umpteen cigarette lighters, where a dozen or perhaps fifteen male survivors huddled. There was only one course open to me if I was to reach them and escape. I had to jump. It was to be literally a leap for life. If I missed grabbing onto the stairs at the other side I would plunge to an almost certain death.

I do not claim this was a brave action, or a heroic one; it was simply that I had this overpowering will to survive. There was little time to think of the consequences. I jumped.

I made it and huddled with the others in the illumination of the cigarette lighters. Above us the exit doors were open, and I could see the stars in the night sky. Judging by their haircuts and calm demeanour, most of the men on the stairs were Army personnel in their twenties. They started to lift men out, making steps with clasped hands. I helped get five or six men out, at the same time trying to get my own thoughts together and work out the best course of action. A lesson of the *Lusitania* was that crew were vitally important in getting a rescue started. With my unique knowledge of the ship I could help locate rescue equipment, lifeboats and lifejackets.

I said to one of the lads, 'Excuse me, can I get out so I can get some rescue work organised?' It was agreed, two hands made a step for me, and then I was out of the hull in the cold and biting air.

Other crew members were out too. I saw Mick Mordue getting equipment from the ferry's lifeboats, which there had not been time to launch – axes and torches. We got a knotted lifeline and lowered it into the darkness so the remaining men on the stairwell could get out. There was a bitterly cold East wind, and yet this did not register with me; I still just could not believe that any of it was happening.

Ship's Carpenter Mick Tracey was opening lockers and getting out lifejackets, and I saw an Army officer – who I later learned lost some family – also helping.

The hull was OK to walk on, and as I was crossing it I saw the most bizarre sight. A little boy, aged two, was standing there alone, gazing out towards the lights of Zeebrugge. He looked totally isolated and abandoned. I picked him up and held him tight. He threw his arms tightly around my neck and shoulders. As he did tears started to roll down my cheeks as I thought of my own son Simon, younger than this small child by about six months. Then, amid all that horror and confusion, he pointed at the lights of Zeebrugge and said, 'Look at the pretty lights.'

I followed his gaze. It all looked so normal, just as we had left it such a short time ago. There life went on as before; here, for us, it had changed for ever.

Someone came up and said, 'Shall I hold the boy?' Sharply I replied, 'No'. Somehow I did not want to give him up. I learned later his name was Matthew Conway and he came from Milton Keynes. At the time I was angry with whoever had left him there unattended in such a potentially dangerous place. But I shouldn't have been, as his father Chris had put Matthew on deck with strict instructions not to move, so that Chris could go back and rescue his pregnant wife Debbie. Five minutes later Chris was back with Debbie, and I handed their son back. I remember Debbie crying, 'I've got pains in my stomach.' Luckily she did not give birth then, but had a healthy 7lb 4oz boy, Paul Andrew, just over four weeks later.

I felt stronger now. Something about just clinging to Matthew and holding him had given me new courage, and the power to go on. After he and his parents were taken off by the tugs which were soon at the scene,

I started to think what we could do to get more passengers out.

I do not call what I did in the way of rescuing people heroism or bravery; I call it duty. I was taught that the passengers come first, the crew second. And I believe that each crewman that night put their duty to the passengers before their personal safety if they were at all capable of doing so.

I saw Mark Stanley, the Assistant Bosun, pulling people out of the ship, and cutting his own hands badly in the process. Still desperate, as we all were, to learn why the *Herald* had capsized, I said, 'Christ, Mark, what happened?'

He looked quite ghastly, his face white and clearly shocked. 'The doors! The doors! I left the doors open!' Mark said.

I had absolutely no idea what he was talking about. No idea at all that he had failed to close the massive bow doors, and that the sea had powered in and doomed the *Herald*. He turned away and we both carried on helping with the rescue.

I climbed back into the pitch-black interior of the ship and did my utmost to rescue as many people as I could. Meanwhile I could not help reflecting on how I had found myself here, and what chance of Fate had led me to a ship whose name would join the infamous in the annals of maritime disasters. I thought of the bitter irony of my last Christmas present from my wife Anne, who knows how crazy I am about ships and the sea.

It was a make-it-yourself model of the *Titanic*.

# 2

## *Day Trip*

My association with the sea started for me, as it ended for so many at Zeebrugge, with a day trip across the Channel. Then a random stone played its part, flicked up by the tyres of a sports car on a road in Northern France. Two unconnected events, but they led me inexorably to a career at sea and towards that fateful night.

Although I was born near the sea, in the village of Ore near Hastings in Sussex on 10 June 1952, I did not seem destined to be a sailor. When I was three my father Dennis moved the family to Devon, where he and Mum ran a small farm of sheep, chickens and dairy cattle. One of my earliest memories is of a farmer accidentally shooting a cow, and my mother telling me to close my eyes as they hauled it away. But with the natural curiosity of the young, I peeped, and can still remember that poor carcass as it was hauled ignominiously away. I can remember also seeing Lundy Isle from Westward Ho!, and the amphibious DUKWs 'ducks', those ex-Army river crossers that trundled off the sands and into the sea. How much I wished to go in one, but the nearest I got to being amphibious was sitting in a rowing boat for a short time.

Later we moved to New Romney in Kent, and eventually my father took a shop in Folkestone selling second-hand furniture and antiques.

I got my first proper sea trip – to France – at age 11. I had two brothers; Clifford, three years older than me, and Robin, seven years younger. Robin, then almost five, Mum and Dad, an uncle and my grandmother, and me, went over for the day to Boulogne on the steamer *St Patrick*

In France we took a taxi to the local Commonwealth War Cemetery. My mother's grandfather had served in East Africa and India with the Army in World War I and I think it was that that inspired the visit. It was hard to understand as an 11-year-old that there were the remains of a dead person, just feet away, beneath the lush turf. In fact, in that cemetery there were hundreds of them. Rows upon rows of young men who had died for their country.

It was beyond my comprehension, looking at the names on the headstones, that these had ever been real human beings with lives and loves, with feelings and friends, mother and fathers, and perhaps wives and babies. It would be more than 23 years before *I* was to see violent, sudden and unnecessary death of fellow comrades at close quarters.

We went back into Boulogne and had a meal. I remember being intoxicated by the strange new smells – garlic, fresh bread, wine, pastis, pungent smoke from the Gitanes cigarettes. I still love those unmistakable French smells today.

The return journey was aboard the *Maid of Kent*, and my brother Robin was heartily seasick, although I wasn't. Perhaps there was an omen there. Nothing could spoil that day for me, and the whole trip made a great impact on an impressionable young mind. This was travel, this was adventure, this was what I had read about in comics.

I adored the ships, the smell of the salt air and the sight of the waves. And I was awed by the sailors in their smart uniforms as they went briskly about their duties. Some kids want to be train drivers, or doctors or policemen. But from that trip to France I thought I would like to be a sailor, wear a uniform, sail off to sea and visit exotic foreign places. But I kept those thoughts to myself as that magical day came to an end.

I was then a pupil at Southlands Secondary School in New Romney, and I was not brilliant academically. I am by nature quiet and introverted, and was even then something of a loner.

Neither was I a star sportsman – I loathed cricket especially – preferring instead to read. But I liked history and religion – and geography. I learned about Columbus and the discovery of new lands. I studied Australia and Canada, because in those days geography was biased towards the British Commonwealth, the Dominions and former colonies. I had one wish, and that was to travel to those places, and my chance soon came. I left school at 15, something not uncommon in the mid-Sixties for lads like me.

My yearning for travel was strong, and I discussed with my careers master the possibility of joining the Royal Navy. I even went to Portsmouth to see how things were done in the senior service. I visited barracks and training areas, talked with young recruits, and saw ships from a distance even if I did not get to go aboard. The visit was useful as it gave me the distinct impression that sailors in the Royal Navy, and especially new recruits, spent far too little of their time travelling to foreign climes. And that, after all, was my main imperative.

Next I thought about the Merchant Navy, and eventually I was accepted on a 12-week course at a Merchant Navy school for deck boys at Gravesend, once I reached the age of 16.

It was not a question of them paying you ... *you* paid *them*, £30 if my memory serves me. But the reward, if you passed, was not inconsiderable; you got your Seamen's Record Book, without which you could not put to sea as crew on any British merchant vessel.

There were 500 of us, all lads, living in dormitories, and the discipline was military, if not excessively severe. We called the instructors 'Sir', and we wore a uniform of black shoes, black trousers, white shirt, black tie and a black 'bum-freezer' jacket with brass buttons. Our hat was a black beret with the round, brass badge of the National Sea Training School. For rough work or fatigues we had blue denim shirts and trousers.

There were inspections. On one occasion I was reprimanded because my shirt was allegedly dirty, even though it was freshly washed and ironed. I changed it there and then for a brand-new shirt straight out of the wrapper. The inspecting officer said, 'It's still dirty – but I'll let it go ...'

We rose at six o'clock, waxed and polished the floors, washed, and then had breakfast between seven and eight. Then it was lessons and work, the theory and the practice of being at sea.

As I was on a deck course I learned the 360 points of the compass – boxing the compass we called it – off by heart. We learned the different types of vessels and how to recognise them, we studied maintenance and operation, about derricks and lifeboats, and also McGregor hatches and how to close them. We had drummed into us which was the fo'c'sle and which was the poop deck. We ate lunch between twelve and one, and had tea between five and six. We were in bed by nine and 'lights out' by ten. Most of us were shattered anyway.

We sailed on the Medway, learning the hard way about boats and ships, knots, pulleys and water-tight compartments. At night you could hear some of the lads crying in their bunks, and sometimes bunks emptied, their occupants no longer able to take any more. Our hair had been shorn on our arrival, and the word was that they put bromide in your tea, just in case you had energy left for libidinous outlets.

I loved every minute of it. I went home on Christmas leave in my uniform feeling very proud. On 28 February 1969, at age 16½, I passed my exams, coming second out of a class of 30.

I had achieved my prized light-blue Seamen's Record Book and my number, R.870416. It meant I was qualified for Home Trade and Deep Sea articles, as the Merchant Navy describes them. A sea voyage from Liverpool to Glasgow, for example, is classed as Home Trade; Liverpool to Rio, Deep Sea.

On the last day of training we lined up on a big square and were given the good wishes of the men who had pushed us so hard during those weeks.

Later I took a train to London and presented myself at the offices of the Shipping Federation in Prescot Street, close to the Aldgate East Underground station. There I was interviewed and reminded that as a member of the proud British Merchant Marine, I should do my duty faithfully and obey orders. I was then issued with my National Sea Training School Certificate of Proficiency. I was told to go home, and that I would be informed by a telegram when a place on a ship was available.

At last the telegram arrived, and I opened it feverishly. 'Report with gear nine a.m. Monday next, Southampton, to join cargo ship *Sussex*. Shipping Federation.'

This, I thought, was it. Now I would see the world.

I had an old kitbag, and I stowed my gear in it and eagerly caught the train for Southampton. The reality was a little disillusioning. She was a cargo ship of about 9,000 tons, bound for Glasgow with frozen lamb and bales of wood. My first trip would be Home Trade.

The *Sussex* had a mainly Scottish crew, rough and ready but good-humoured, and they took fatherly care of the young innocent who had joined them. We went off down the Channel, round Cornwall, up past Liverpool and the Isle of Man, and on up to Scotland. On the voyage I got the job of being the ship's 'Peggy', the lad who lays the table, serves the food, and ... cleans out the toilets!

I had never been to Glasgow, and I found it lived up to its reputation as a tough city. I went into a pub for a drink, where a suspicious barman asked my age. I lied, telling him I was 18. He flung me out anyway; I had not known the legal age for drinking in Scotland was 21!

But I was soon to get what I longed for, and it was not a drink. It was Deep Sea – an overseas voyage. We were bound for New Zealand via Curacao in the West Indies, and the Panama Canal.

We got to Curacao and I thought 'This is the life'. We went ashore and there was calypso, Dutch beer, and beautiful girls who danced to music from the juke-box. And outside in the sultry night air there was the sound of crickets. It was everything I had ever dreamed of when I had pored over my geography books at school, and I felt very grown-up. When we put to sea again it was so hot that we slept out on deck on mattresses. It was humid with hardly any breeze, so the cabin that four of us shared was unbearably stuffy.

As new deck boy I had all the usual sea tricks pulled on me. They sent me for a left-handed spanner or a tin of spotted paint, or asked me to save any spare bread for the mules that pulled the ships through the Panama Canal. As I quickly learned, the 'mules' were mechanical tractors that had been given that name. I remember still the Canal itself, with its plaque commemorating the number of men who died for every foot of the man-made waterway when it was being constructed. I remember palm trees, Americans in white shorts, lush vegetation.

Next it was into the Pacific, and I saw my first flying fish, skimming through the water alongside the boat. We crossed the Equator on 23 April 1969. We had engine trouble, and to pass away the idle hours while they were being fixed, some of us went shark fishing. It was crude stuff with just a rope, a butcher's hook, and a piece of raw meat. But it brought me face to face with my own private *Jaws!* We got one up as far as the rail, but when I tried to haul it over I came *too* close for comfort to those fearsome teeth. Horrible! At that point the line broke and it fell back into the sea, and I was very glad.

We passed Tahiti on 1 May, and the islands were like a dream in the distance; everything you have ever imagined with palm trees waving lazily against a flame-red sunset and a distinctive aroma drifting out to the ship of coconuts and copra.

Our arrival in Auckland, New Zealand, was very

raunchy, as a bevy of local girls greeted the ship by lowering their skirts and panties, and flashing their bare bottoms at us as we docked. Later we all went to a bar called the Snakepit, where I met a very pretty girl and had my first serious, if necessarily brief, romance.

We returned the same way that we had come, and on 10 June, as we were crossing the International Dateline, I celebrated my 17th birthday. Returning the way we did meant that we gained a day, so I had *two* birthdays. I hope that does not add a year to my age.

Our next trip was to Japan via Freetown, Sierra Leone in Africa, and Dampier in Australia. At Freetown we were besieged with offers from the locals. Girls? Boys? Dope? Whatever they thought we wanted they offered. A paint-spattered nylon shirt could get you a bunch of bananas from the boys on the so-called 'bumboats' that darted around the ship like shoals of pilot fish. We declined the girls and the other offers, and settled instead for a tour ashore. The highspot for the guide and the rest of my shipmates was when I accidentally stepped into a newly dug village latrine. I did not smell so good for quite a while!

It was on the return voyage, en route to Vitoria, near Rio de Janeiro in Brazil, that an incident occurred which affected me deeply, and which was to echo in my mind during those harrowing hours aboard the *Herald of Free Enterprise* off Zeebrugge.

We were in the South China Sea, off the southern coast of Taiwan, when we went to the aid of a tanker, the *Sofia*, that had broken its back in heavy seas. We were told to make ready safety netting for survivors to climb aboard, and to prepare medical supplies and bunks for the rescued crew.

Our ship closed on the broken stern part of the stricken vessel, where the crew had gathered at the after end. As we moved closer we could see a couple of stretcher cases, and could hear men screaming. We kept closing, and then veering away. And we did this for a total of 12 hours without making – in the crew's opinion – a determined attempt to get alongside and rescue the crew. We knew that the fractured portion of ship could not stay afloat for ever, and at one point there was a near-mutiny when the crew talked, purely among ourselves, of lowering a lifeboat without the permission of the Master. We felt that the least we could do was try to fire a line over to them, and get a breeches buoy rigged to get the crew over to us.

Eventually a United States Navy warship appeared and took command of the rescue, instructing us to leave the scene.

The next day we learned that the stern of the severed tanker had sunk eventually with the loss of 12 men. We felt very badly about the whole incident, as if we had failed as British Merchant seamen, with a proud tradition, to make a determined effort to rescue those men.

This earlier mishap was much in my mind when I went back into the interior of the *Herald* on that bitterly cold March night. I knew that I could not have lived with myself if I had made no attempt to rescue those poor trapped people.

The occurrence in the South China Sea also brought home a very important message to me. This was that however big and impressive the ship, the sea was *always* infinitely more powerful, and it had a way of punishing pride and arrogance. The ship was your home, but it was not a secure home, moving as it did through an alien and always potentially dangerous environment. I stood at the stern of a ship once, and saw the bow moving in relation to the rest of the ship. It was nothing to be alarmed about in itself. Just as aeroplanes bend and move in the air, so do ships at sea. In fact, it is precisely this 'give' which prevents them from snapping like twigs. But seeing that movement reminded me that this new home of mine was constantly moving and adapting to its ever-changing surroundings.

I realised that one could never be totally safe here; the sea was cruel and it could kill, as I had so recently seen. And unlike Man, the sea never slept.

In Brazil we went ashore to a village called Sebastian, where I saw the most beautiful olive-skinned girls I have ever seen. No one was terribly wealthy, but everyone seemed happy and radiant with good health. One girl, whose name was Rowena, took a fancy to me and began to follow me around. Eventually it all became a little difficult, and the police had to be called.

But gradually I realised that things were beginning to change in the Merchant Navy, in fact *had* changed, even in the relatively short period I had been at sea. Ships were getting bigger, ports of call fewer, and less and less time was actually being spent in port. Terminals were being built to unload the new big container vessels, and now it was possible to unload cargo without ever getting close to the harbour. You could sail all the way somewhere on the other side of the world, turn around in two or three days, and never set foot on land. I had joined the Merchant Navy for travel and exotic locations, not just to be stuck aboard ship for weeks on end, eventually only to stare at the very country I wanted to see.

I joined the *Sagacity* for a while, a small coaster taking loose grain up to Preston. Once, during rough weather, I was asked to go into the hold and put grain into sacks to form a barrier to stop the rest of it from shifting. As I worked at this task, the *Sagacity* swerved as another vessel cut dangerously across our bows. Immediately the grain began to shift toward me like a vast sea, and I thought I was about to be buried alive. Luckily it stopped, and I worked on for another three hours. When I came out I was frightened and very shaky.

Sadly, though, the writing was on the wall concerning the future of the merchant service, and reluctantly I left, turning my back on the sea, I thought for ever.

It was a freak accident on a road outside Lille in Northern France that was to lead to a new career at sea, and inevitably to Zeebrugge.

But first it seemed, the sea was not done with me. And I have wondered since, not in the least flippantly, whether it was out to get me. It was 1971, and I was working for a small engineering firm in New Romney. Six of us decided to hire a van, drive to Newquay in Cornwall, and go surfing. At the beach I was having a great time riding the waves. But I kept falling off and was spending ages retrieving my surfboard, so I decided to secure my surfboard by a link to my ankle as some surfers do.

This decision saved my life. There are strange currents on that stretch of sea, and as a wave threw me off my board, a strong current pulled me under. I tried to fight my way to the surface but the current was just too strong. I went under twice, swallowing water, my lungs filling with it. I was choking, and just an ace from drowning.

Then luckily the buoyancy of the surfboard shot it to the surface, and it yanked me with it like a cork. I beached coughing and choking, vomiting water, and fighting for breath. My legs felt like jelly and I was very frightened. I had really believed that my end had come. Yet I surfed again that holiday. Crazy.

At that time I was rootless and unsettled. I went up to stay with my brother Clifford in Brixton, South London, where he was in a rock band called Raw Material. I worked with them as an electrician and learnt the trade as I went along, finally even rewiring houses – luckily the others were experts so no one was electrocuted because of me.

But I still thought about the sea, and at weekends would go down to Folkestone, and up onto the cliffs to gaze out over the English Channel. I wondered about the ships, their tonnage, what they were carrying, and tried to identify the types from the profile of their hull and superstructure. I suppose this was the lure of the sea.

When I left Brixton for good, I worked for an engineering firm for 18 months, and then applied for work as a welder at Dungeness Nuclear Power Station. It was to be the most depressing time of my life. To see that monstrosity from the bus, looming out of the mist like some science fiction creation, was awful. I had seen Africa, the West Indies, Brazil, New Zealand; and now my horizon was bordered by a nuclear power station.

Germany now called to me. The firm of Depike Engineers of Hamburg wanted welders, and I was eager to go. I was by then the proud owner of a 1965 MGB roadster in British racing green, with wire wheels, which I had bought in 1973 for £265, and which I lavished with affection and attention. In August 1974 I drove it to Harwich, put us both on the German ferry *Prinz Hamlet* and made the 24-hour crossing to Hamburg.

My home was a pig-farm, Dorfstrasse 5, Kisdorf, and there were three other lodgers: a Londoner, a Lancastrian and a Lithuanian. We started work each morning at 7-30 sharp, with a 30-minute break at noon. We were making power station components destined for the Soviet Union. Sometimes the foreman, Manfred Faulkner, who had learned his English from the occupying American troops shortly after the war, would insist that I go home and meet his family. He had a picture which he used to thrust forward at visitors. It was Adolf Hitler with a young lad. Who, Manfred would ask, is the boy? It was, of course, Manfred.

I had a trip to Berlin with an au pair I had befriended, and after a trip home for Christmas, went back to Germany with a mate who suggested that we could make more money working on US bases around Frankfurt. We couldn't, though. The trip was a disaster, and I returned to England in March 1975, extremely short of money. I decided to take the MGB on the cheapest sea crossing to Calais, and then drive to Hamburg to try and take up again where I had left off.

This was where Fate took a hand. While driving earlier I had heard a 'clunk' and, as I approached the suburbs of Lille in the growing dusk, the engine began to overheat and the temperature gauge needle crept quickly into the danger zone. I pulled over as smoke and steam belched from the bonnet, and water leaked from the radiator. A check revealed that the 'clunk' I had heard was an errant stone flying up and hitting the fan blade. The blade had bent out of line and sliced into the radiator.

Had this happened *after* I reached Hamburg there would have been no problem, for the city boasts an MG garage. But in Lille, it was hopeless. A kind Frenchman stopped and tried to help. Eventually he gave me a welcome dinner of ham, salad, chips, bread, wine and coffee in his home. But the car could not so easily be restored.

I spent the night in a hotel, put filler in the radiator

and the next morning limped back to Calais, the big-ends knocking because of the constant overheating.

When I got the MGB home I could not afford to have it repaired; and sadly I sold it for £50, which almost broke my heart. I had no job, no car, and I was completely skint. My aim was to get a job, save some more money and go back to Germany.

Then the local paper, the *Folkestone Herald*, ran a story that the cross-channel ferry company Townsend Thoresen were offering seasonal work as Assistant Stewards. In some ways a job like this would be a come down. I was already an experienced seaman, and I had sailed as far as Japan. Now I was to be – well, let's be frank – a waiter on a ship sailing the 22 miles between Dover and Calais and back again.

But I was glad. It was a job, they would pay me, and there would probably be tips. But most of all, in my heart of hearts, I knew that I was back at sea where I belonged.

# 3

# *Safety*

As an Assistant Steward I wore a white jacket with blue-green lapels, and took orders and served food in the restaurant of the *Free Enterprise 2* on the Dover–Calais run. The tips were good, and I was saving the money I still thought I would put towards my return journey to Germany. But rapidly the sea was getting back into my blood.

I became head waiter before the season ended and staff are normally paid off, and was asked to stay on, so in September 1975 I joined the *Free Enterprise 5* as a member of the permanent Townsend Thoresen crew.

Everyone is an expert on ferry safety now. Suddenly everyone can spot the abuses and the obvious faults. But even then I began to see worrying lapses of safety on board that disquieted me. For example, one day on board *Free Enterprise 2* we were trying to have a lifeboat drill in Dover harbour. I say 'try' because the whole thing degenerated into farce.

A 40-person liferaft of the inflatable type was dropped into the water, to await the yank on a line which inflates it. But it took two officers, one of them the Master of the vessel, about five minutes before the liferaft finally inflated. Then catering staff were supposed to climb down into it, simulating an abandon ship procedure, but within seconds of the first crew getting in, there was an anguished female shriek. The raft was leaking. Perhaps it was old, or out of date, in need of repair, or perhaps it had been vandalised, I do not know. At the time everyone saw the funny side of it, but I saw the serious side of the incident, too.

Suppose we had been sinking in mid-Channel, in a gale, instead of just carrying out an exercise in the tranquillity of Dover harbour? Suppose that instead of experienced crew clambering into the liferaft, there had been actual passengers, including the elderly, women with babies in their arms and young children?

The fixed liferafts on board ships, the ones that hang from davits – the ones that actually *look* like lifeboats – have a bung in them, which is a sort of plug. When the lifeboat is hung up, the bung is removed and stored nearby. This is done to stop the boat filling up with rainwater. So the first job before lowering the lifeboats is to locate the bung and replace it in the boat. But I found that frequently bungs were left in, and that lifeboats had collected rainwater when they came to be lowered.

There was, and still is, intense pressure on ships' Masters and crew, to get the ship from A to B according to a strict timetable, then turn it around and bring it back. Delays mean dissatisfied customers and an unhappy company. That pressure, the omnipresent time factor, mitigated against regular safety drills. There was supposed to be one major crew lifeboat drill every third week, but in my experience at least one in six were cancelled.

Drills were supposed to be sprung upon us as a complete surprise. That was the point, as after all we would not be forewarned in a real emergency at sea. But frequently a Second Officer or Deck Officer would say, 'Lifeboat drill when we get to Calais (or Zeebrugge) ... pass it on.' Then, as often as not, that drill would be cancelled because we were late turning around.

Every drill should involve crew going to the Muster station. Each person is assigned a function for emergencies, some manning stretchers, some First-Aid packs, others supervising passengers. But because of changes in duty rosters, individuals often did not know their particular function on any given watch, unless they checked it specifically – as they were required to do – with the Muster list when they came aboard. Sadly, few did, and the drills that *were* held resulted in total confusion, with people running around willy-nilly, not knowing what they were supposed to be doing.

Once, when I was first learning the job of Assistant Purser, I was counting the tickets, that is the number of people we had on board, and realised that we had too many people on board. I said, 'The figure is over – we're overloaded.' And the Master at the time replied, 'Lose some tickets.' These extra tickets were literally taken and thrown overboard.

Masters of vessels – the public would call them the Captain – were just that, masters. What they said went. There was a class system aboard ship and Masters were at the apex of the triangle whose base was the deck crew. Masters rarely spoke to the rest of us; they earned an incredible amount of money – to the rest of us, anyway – and of course they had a tremendous responsibility. But many Masters believed they always knew best, and on occasions they took risks we felt were unjustified.

One such incident happened on the *Free Enterprise 5*. The ship had just come from a re-fit in Flushing, Holland, and was to depart Zeebrugge for Dover with just a little freight and a few lorry drivers on board. The weather was appalling, the sea storm-tossed, and in spite of warnings from the Zeebrugge Port Authority we put to sea. A journey that should have taken four and a half hours took 20. It was so rough that it became impossible to stand up. When the *Free Enterprise 5* finally limped into port it was found that lorry trailers had overturned on the cargo deck causing thousands of pounds worth of damage. It took a crane and a forklift truck to clear them.

But not all of the safety lapses could be laid at the feet of the company or the Masters. Sometimes these Masters, who had so much authority, did not use it. Often they failed to stamp their brand of discipline and order on their ship. Each ship would have at least five

Masters, because of the round-the-clock sailings. In the early Seventies seamen had the power to put a ship 'against the wall' – that is, refuse to sail it unless some small fault was rectified or some grievance settled to their satisfaction. Masters feared that power.

So on the one hand they could be martinets, checking a door top in the Catering Department, looking for a speck of dirt. On the other they would ignore a 'deckie' asleep in his bunk because they were frightened of the repercussions if they reprimanded him.

I was a member of the National Union of Seamen, and I am definitely not anti-union. But when I eventually became an Assistant Purser, it was an ongoing battle against some of the extreme Left troublemakers.

One problem was drink, and its availability on the ferry and its low cost. I am not teetotal, and I do enjoy a drink myself; but I believe drink has caused serious discipline problems on some cross-channel ferries.

Crew members get a pink or white Crew Issue Voucher which entitles them, for example, to buy half a bottle of vodka for 70 pence. Unless the person was going on leave that drink could not be taken ashore; in other words, it had to be consumed on board. The obvious happened, and men drank far more than was safe for themselves or their charges while on duty on a ship at sea.

One seaman actually threatened a couple of Assistant Pursers, who backed off, frightened. He was a big bloke, and incidentally a very pleasant man and a good worker when sober. But on this particular day in the Mess, he was swearing, using four-letter words and generally making himself thoroughly objectionable. He was clearly very drunk, and when I told him to watch his language he threatened to 'sort me out'. I refused to retreat, and told him that if he wished to lose his job, he could go ahead and support his words with action. He backed off, but was later sacked for some other offence. It was just one example of the dangers of allowing crew to drink cheap booze on duty.

Another far more serious incident occurred on the *Free Enterprise 5* in 1980. It was well-known that the engineers had a beer club; they had a barrel, and would note down each pint they took out, and that amount would be deducted from their booze allowance. Normally they would wait until they got into port and the engines were off before they got stuck in. But on one particular day they were dangerously premature.

On that day I believe they had had a few beers on the trip over. For as the ship waited outside the Eastern dock, ready to berth, the engineering lads actually thought the ship had berthed ... and they switched off the engines, left the engine room, went to their quarters and began showering and breaking out the beer! It was a potentially lethal situation, as the ship was drifting, without power, towards the harbour wall, without any of the passengers realising it. The horrified Master put out a Tannoy for the engineers to contact the bridge, as the Master's calls to the engine room were going unanswered. The engineers heard the announcement, contacted the bridge, and then dashed back to the engine room and restarted the engines. Disaster was averted. I understand the matter was dealt with internally, but it should be recorded in the ship's log. I *know* it happened, because I was on board at the time.

But far more serious than all this – as has now been proved with such shattering consequences – was the matter of the car-door entrance at the bow of the ships. On the earlier breed of cross-channel ferries, the bow door hinged upwards like the visor on a medieval knight's helmet. Standing on the bridge the Master could clearly see when the door was open, but just as clearly, and more importantly, that it had been closed. Later ships, like the *Herald of Free Enterprise*, which came into service on 29 May 1980, had bow doors that opened outwards. It was impossible to tell from the bridge whether they were open or shut.

Incredibly, as we now know, Masters had nothing to tell them – no video camera system, or warning lights – whether the bow doors were open or shut. The negative system applied: unless told otherwise the Master *assumed* the doors had been closed. The reasoning behind this assumption was that there was a man responsible for checking the doors, and also someone else to see that he did it. So nothing could go wrong, could it?

I knew, as the public has since learned from the official inquiry into the *Herald* tragedy, that various memos had been sent by Masters to Townsend Thoresen, urging that a system of visual or electronic surveillance be installed as a safety measure. Effectively these were ignored.

A word too about the design of the later breed of ships, of which the *Herald* was one. In the event of them capsizing they were death traps, because everything had been designed to keep people *inside* the superstructure.

The old vessels had far more deck space around the sides of the ship. The newer vessels, like the *Herald*, were walled in, with large reinforced windows as portholes, flush with the side of the hull. Perhaps the designers or the company would say the aim was to give people more warmth in a Northern climate, reasoning that few people like to go out on deck during a Channel crossing. We below decks believed that the aim of the later design was to encourage people to stay indoors and spend money in the arcades, the bars, the cafeterias and restaurants, and the Duty Free shops.

Had it been an older-style ferry that capsized that night off Zeebrugge, I believe it would have been far easier for people to escape. But no one designs a ship or an aeroplane with a worst-case scenario uppermost in their mind. And no one, myself included, really thinks about it until the worst has actually happened.

# 4

# *List to Port*

After a stint on the *Free Enterprise 5* I was transferred to the *Free Enterprise 7* as Head Waiter on the Zeebrugge run. Frankly I did not like it. On the 5 there seemed to be pride in the ship; on the 7, there was very little. It was also clear that the Senior Purser – the man responsible for catering staff – had no intention of recommending any of us for promotion, however deserved.

We used to have about an hour and a half in Zeebrugge on each run, and some of us used to bring bicycles, or borrow them there, and ride into town and have a beer. I sailed in and out of that port countless times, but never in my worst nightmares did I envisage what lay ahead for me years in the future outside that very port.

At last a new Senior Purser was appointed, called Neville Good. He recommended two or three of us for long-overdue promotions, and so I became an Assistant Purser.

On some runs there would be two Assistant Pursers, on other runs three. On the *Herald*, for example, for each 24-hour watch (or shift, if you like) there were three of us: one on the Information Office – my job on that terrible night – one running the catering and selling points, the third in charge of the bonded stores.

Our uniform was black trousers, a double-breasted black tunic with two rows of brass buttons inscribed with the words 'Merchant Navy' and a band on the sleeve, and a hat. The peaked cap had a dark peak, a white top, and a badge of a crown with laurel leaves and the letters TT (Townsend Thoresen) in gold.

I had worked hard for this, and was very proud to have achieved it. I was back at sea performing a useful function; and my private life had taken a turn for the better too. I have always been a singular sort of chap, and I thought perhaps that I would never marry. Then in 1981 I met Anne, a slim, dark-haired Dover girl, who was doing a season as a stewardess with Townsend Thoresen. At the end of that season she left, and went to work for National Car Rental in Dover, but our relationship continued. Four years later we were married on 11 May at Dover Register Office, just three minutes walk from the docks.

It was on a plane going to Austria for a skiing holiday that I learned I was to be a father. I had urged Anne to have a glass of wine to celebrate the start of our holiday. She said that she couldn't, not that she wouldn't, but that she *couldn't*. I still did not understand, and pressed her to have something alcoholic – and then at last it dawned. I said 'You're not?', and she said 'I am'. I was overjoyed, and spent the whole holiday rushing to her side solicitously if she so much as stumbled. Now I have my lovely, adorable Simon, with his blond hair and cheeky face, and it makes me wonder how I ever managed without marriage and fatherhood.

Two months after my wedding I was transferred to the *Herald of Free Enterprise*. From the moment I set foot on board that ship it was clear to me that the vessel had a distinct, if not pronounced, list to port. In plain language she was not perpendicular; she leaned over to the left. As a result water that would normally clear from the scuppers would collect there, and when there was a pronounced roll, the water would slosh out onto the galley floor. A dishwasher whose first name was John, a member of A Watch, slipped in that excess water and was concussed. An American doctor who happened to be travelling, treated him.

The list was perhaps not more than a couple of degrees, and it is likely that most passengers never noted it. Whenever I asked *why* the ship listed, no one seemed able to give me an answer. At the official inquiry into the *Herald* disaster, the list was referred to. For when the *Herald* sailed from Zeebrugge with the bow doors open, it was bow down in the water and listing to port, the side to which it ultimately capsized.

I am not trying to be wise after the event, but I think someone should have discovered at the beginning, exactly why the *Herald* had a list, and then corrected it.

There were other reasons why my initial move to the *Herald* was an unhappy one. There were lots of militants on board who wanted things done their way, and if you tried to exercise your authority they tried to undermine it. There was no flexibility, and all agreements had to be written down and strictly adhered to, to the letter.

At one point the Assistant Pursers agreed that we would move catering staff around where possible, giving people the chance to try other jobs, so that one person did not get stuck doing the washing up all the time. We also suspected that one or two of the catering staff were on the fiddle, and we felt that rotating staff would help combat that problem. A Steward or Assistant Steward can be moved. It is within the rules of his or her employment, and we had the right and the authority to do this.

But we faced a real battle. People would claim they had other classifications for their tasks, which meant it was vital they stayed where they were. It became a struggle which lasted months, with people playing one off against the other. It was an ongoing battle just to get people to do the job they were supposed to be doing, and it really got to me. I used to lie in bed sleepless at nights.

Eventually I transferred to C Watch, where I settled in much better, making close and dear friends, some of whom would perish at Zeebrugge. Had I stayed on A Watch I would not have been at Zeebrugge, and my life would not have been altered totally and utterly.

# 5

# *Just Another Day*

Friday, 6 March 1987, promised to be just another day. On Monday the *Herald* was due to go into dock for a re-fit, and I was taking leave. Anne and I planned to spend it doing some decorating in the semi-detached house we had bought on Folkestone's Canterbury Road. I can remember, and such details seem incredibly important afterwards, that we had chosen a gold-striped wallpaper for the living room.

The *Herald*'s re-fit was to have been more than a paste and paper DIY job. Because there was more freight and fewer passengers on the Zeebrugge run, it had been decided to rip out a bar, cafeteria and 'salad bowl' serving area, and install reclining seats.

That day we were supposed to make two round trips to Zeebrugge during my 24-hour duty period as Assistant Purser in charge of the Information Office. The radio alarm woke me at 7-30 a.m.; I got out of bed, put on a towelling bathrobe, went downstairs and put on a kettle for tea. I came back upstairs, switched on our bedroom TV, tuned to TV-AM and went through to Simon's bedroom. He was already awake, standing up in his cot looking sleepy but lovable in his blue sleepsuit. I took him into our room and tucked him in next to Anne, before going back downstairs. I poured the boiling water on our favourite tea bags, put sugar in my tea, and prepared some orange cordial in a plastic beaker for Simon. Holding the mugs in one hand with the beaker in the other, I padded barefoot back upstairs and climbed into bed with Anne and Simon, and watched the early-morning news.

It was our regular routine, cosy and familiar. There was nothing to suggest that it should not go on like that for years. We were not even middle-aged yet. We were all in good health. There was nothing, not even on the news bulletin, to disturb the feeling of well-being and security engendered by lying snug with your wife and child beneath the bedclothes, sipping the day's first cup of tea.

Before I bathed and washed my hair, while listening to Derek Jameson's Radio 2 show on the transistor we keep in the bathroom, I first went to the kitchen and ironed a shirt. For the 24-hour shift I use two, taking a spare with me.

I dressed: black polished shoes, black trousers, white shirt, black socks, company epaulettes. Simon gurgled contentedly, and Anne and I chatted about the decorating, and my brother Clifford, who was coming over to visit us from Canada where he now lived. And excitedly we went over the plans for our own trip to Canada in May. We had already bought three tickets for the flight to Toronto.

I took my leather shoulder bag that I had bought on holiday in Rhodes, and packed the extra shirt, and papers, memos and British Rail timetable that I needed to assist the passengers. I also grabbed the flat cap I used going to and fro to work. We hardly ever wore our peaked caps except for important occasions.

By this time Anne and Simon were up and dressed. Normally we would kiss goodbye at the door, I would give Simon a cuddle, and then we waved to each other as I drove off in our second-hand red Vauxhall Cavalier. Anne and I have always made it a point never to part on a bad note; we had agreed that it would be terrible if something happened to either of us and our last words had been angry ones.

At the many funerals I attended after Zeebrugge, I overheard widows saying, 'Thank God we didn't have a row before he went.' And I actually heard one anguished person say that she and her loved one had bad words before he left, never to return.

As chance would have it that day, Anne drove me the nine miles to Dover's Eastern Docks. So I had that much more precious time with my wife and son. I was to need every memory of love and beautiful moments in the horrendous time to come.

It was spitting with rain, but not enough to make the windscreen wipers necessary, and although it was cold, the prospect of the day ahead was not an unpleasant one. There was no feeling of foreboding, no inkling at all of what was to come, no sixth sense of danger. It was just another normal day on a voyage I had made hundreds of times before. I have experienced exceptionally rough weather, with waves crashing over the bow, and I have sailed in the biggest, most dangerous oceans in the world. Today the sea was moderate. What could there possibly be to fear?

I have a pass to get into Eastern Docks, but our faces had become so familiar to the policemen on duty at the gate that they rarely noticed us, and so it was that day.

I like getting to work a little early to give myself a head start on things. It also gives me complete justification for giving others a rollicking if they are late. I walked to the number five berth waiting area where the *Herald* was due to tie up at 10-30 – ten minutes away. The *Herald* was a little late, and it was at about 10-40, that I saw it nose into the harbour, go astern and inch into the berth as lines snaked across from the dockside. The crew on that watch started to come off. I saw some cooks I knew by sight, and called 'Hello'. I boarded the *Herald* a couple of minutes later.

It was my job to check which crew were present and which, if any, had reported sick, and which were on leave. Earlier that week, a Steward named John Sproat, a man in his late twenties, had asked to take the Friday 24-hour watch off as he had some domestic problems. I had the right to say no and insist he worked, but I had allowed it. Thus John, who has a small child, missed

Zeebrugge. He later thanked me for possibly saving his life.

Another man, Sean Maynard, was due leave but wanted to save his time for when his wife had their soon-expected child. I had to insist he took the leave, and frankly Sean was very brassed off about it, and at the time I was not his most popular person. In the event his wife went into labour that week anyway, so my decision became academic as he would have missed Zeebrugge anyway.

I also insisted that another Steward, John Parsons, take leave. So he was off-watch too that fateful Friday; afterwards he was incredibly grateful. One man, Ray Parker, was on sick leave after falling off a ladder. Capricious Fate was dictating destinies.

There were three Assistant Pursers on that trip: myself in the Information Office, Charles Smith running the catering, and my good friend David Disbury in charge of bonded stores and selling points. Charles and I survived; Dave died.

Our Senior Purser for that trip was Brian Eades. Brian was a golf fanatic, and we had a brief chat about sport before coming on board. Brian died at Zeebrugge.

We were scheduled for an 11-30 sailing, with the passengers coming aboard at 11 a.m. The trip to Zeebrugge would take four and a half hours. Then we would disembark the passengers and vehicles, and embark the new ones. We should have been back in Dover by 10-30 that night. Then we would repeat the procedure, and I would come off duty at 10-30 the following morning.

The passengers came aboard in good spirits, and I noticed that there were more foot passengers than were usual on the Zeebrugge run, which is normally made up mainly of motorists and lorry drivers. But under a promotional scheme between the *Sun* newspaper and Townsend Thoresen, they were making the return trip for just £1. That allowed them to make quite a profit on the trip, as they could stock up with Duty Free goods on board, and perhaps even cheap food and wine during the brief stop in Belgium. It was a day out at a bargain price.

I remember them laughing and joking, looking forward to the day ahead. I noticed a small group of either black or Asian people, distinguished probably because of the fact that there were so few of them. And I saw some people in wheelchairs, one of whom was the woman whose shocked features I would later see in terrifying circumstances.

My first question from a member of the public was that of a kid of 12 asking me what videos we had on board. I told him we would show two feature films and a Looney Tunes cartoon. On that particular crossing we usually kept five feature films on the ship.

As foot passengers, cars and freight came on board, they were counted, and I was given a copy of each manifest, as this list is called. When I received the manifest I would total up the numbers, then 'walkie-talkie' that figure ashore, including in the information the number of crew on board, and the name of the Master, who was in this case David Lewry. The crew list is then printed out by computer, put in an envelope and sent ashore.

The bridge makes a public announcement over the Tannoy: 'The ship will be sailing for Zeebrugge in ten minutes. Will all those not wishing to sail please go ashore.' Five minutes before we were actually due to sail I put on a cassette tape for broadcast on the Tannoy. In five languages – English, French, German, Flemish and Dutch – it announced: 'Can I have your attention please. This vessel, the *Herald of Free Enterprise*, is about to sail for Zeebrugge. Any persons not sailing, please go ashore.'

The Tannoy came to life again: 'Harbour stations. Stand by fore and aft.' We were ready to leave.

The *Herald* inched slowly away from number five berth, out into the harbour and the cold grey waters of the English Channel. Out we went, past the chalk-white cliffs of Dover, that famous landmark, and on towards Belgium.

The ship and 188 people would never see Dover again.

I put another tape into the giant cassette machine linked to the Tannoy system. In five languages the message announced, 'The Captain, officers and crew would like to welcome you on board the *Herald of Free Enterprise* ...' It was known as the welcome-on-board tape, and it went on to say that the bars, restaurants and Duty Free shops were now open.

There was an immediate rush for the bar. It was

obvious that many of the day trippers were out to enjoy themselves in the traditional way, by having a few drinks. There were no bad scenes or upsetting behaviour, although later on in the voyage one man in his twenties slipped on the stairs after having had a few, and cut his head. I hold a First Aid certificate, and I treated him, dabbing the cut with antiseptic and putting a sticking plaster over it. He said 'Cheers mate', and did not seem too upset. He was one of the *Sun* travellers, and I do not know if he lived or died when the accident happened. Like many other thoughts concerning the tragedy, this one still haunts me.

Townsend Thoresen ran a Junior Sailors Club. Youngsters were given a blue card and a mock-up ship's log that could be signed by the Assistant Purser at the Information Office, thus proving they had made the journey. Each card, for which they had to apply by mail, had their passport-size picture affixed to it, and on each trip they made, each official stamp and signature allowed them to move up a rank from Able Seaman to Captain. Promotion in the Junior Sailors Club was quite speedy; just five complete trips and you were Master of the vessel.

Three boys of about eight or nine, their parents hovering anxiously behind, nervously approached my office, clutching their Junior Sailors Club cards. I took each one, and with my special stamp, printed, 'Junior Sailor' in the space provided. I then wrote 'Dover–Zeebrugge', together with the date, 6 March 1987, and my initials.

I chatted to the boys briefly, and then off they went,

proudly carrying the proof of their trip. I do not know if they were day trippers or whether they continued their journey from Zeebrugge. I have no way of knowing if they are alive or dead, and I wish I did. I cannot for the life of me remember their names.

The sea was calm, and at about 1-15 p.m., when I was relieved by David Disbury, I went up to the Petty Officers' Mess on the deck above B Deck on which I worked. I had roast meat, potatoes, vegetables, and a cup of coffee. On occasions I have had a beer with my lunch, but I did not that day. The Steward who served me was Dave Santer, a slim-built man in his fifties who I had known all the time I had been on the *Herald*'s C Watch. Dave died at Zeebrugge.

The Senior Purser, Brian Eades, asked to see me, and among other things we discussed where on the ship we could store and sell cases of beer. Many people took trips to France or Belgium simply for the purpose of buying case upon case of beer that were far cheaper than in England. We thought we should stock it and sell it too, and were sure that this would be popular with passengers, because then they would not have to lug it around town before they got back on the boat.

We were joined by Steward Ken Hollingsbee, a National Union of Seamen representative, and by the other two Assistant Pursers, David Disbury and Charles Smith. We spoke then about the upcoming re-fit, and sat in Brian's cabin on the ship's port side – the side that went into the water. Brian and David would die that night; Charles, Ken and I would survive.

It was ironic that David should be on the watch at all. The previous October some Assistant Pursers had moved around, but David for some reason had stayed on that particular watch. If he had joined another watch he would have lived. It seemed to me afterwards that our fates had been decided by the toss of some random dice, or the spin of a roulette wheel. If *this* had happened, or if only *that* had not occurred, this person would have lived, and that one would have died.

The talk was friendly and good-natured. We all got on well, and David was a particular friend. We felt that we had worked hard to get where we were. We earned the same (about £13,500 a year), and we both had wives and young children.

David lived over in Dover, and because of the nature of shift patterns, we did not get time to socialise a great deal. But in January a group of us had gone out for a meal with our wives. In all there were eight crew members and their wives. We had a smashing meal, tucking into fish, steaks, drank red and white wine, and finishing off with coffee and brandies. We joked, talked, laughed, and really enjoyed one another's company. We could not know it, but it was to be a Last Supper. Three of the eight crew at the table that night perished at Zeebrugge; David, Steward John Warwick and Senior Barman Terry Frame. Three women became widows, and young kiddies became fatherless.

I returned to my station in the Information Office. It was quiet and I looked out at some of the passengers. I remember seeing Andrew Parker – who was awarded the George Medal for his heroism – with his Filipino wife, his daughter and some friends. They all sat, quietly chatting to one another.

We reached Zeebrugge safely, and docked at around 4 p.m. Greenwich Mean Time, one hour later local time. We were due to sail two hours later at 6 p.m. Greenwich Mean Time, 7 local time.

The computer printout of the crew list, including dates of birth, position on board, and seaman's book number, was handed to the Belgian immigration authorities when we docked. That day it was David Disbury's job to go up to the ship's office, tap the information into the computer and get a printout.

Through our walkie-talkies we were told through which of the ship's doorways the foot passengers would disembark. We announced 'Number One' over the Tannoy and then physically led the foot passengers off.

One said to me cheerfully, 'See you in an hour and a half.'

I estimate there were between 200 and 300 foot passengers who would eventually come back to the ship for the return journey.

Once the passengers were ashore, I was then off duty until 30 minutes before the ship was due to sail again. I went to my cabin for a lie down. The cabin was small but sufficient, with a bunk made up with sheets, a small table and chair, a mirror, wash-basin, four cupboards with coathangers, and some shelves. My leather bag with its odds and ends and spare shirt, was on one shelf. On another was a cassette deck with twin detachable speakers that I had rigged up.

I slipped a tape into the cassette player. It was a compilation I had made up myself of Maria Callas, Luciano Pavarotti, Mozart, and Ronald Byng's Elizabethan Serenade. I lay back and relaxed, letting the opera and classical music wash over me, soothing me. The next time I was to hear Elizabethan Serenade was at Buckingham Palace a year later, when it was played by a small band of the Coldstream Guards as I waited to be awarded the Queen's Gallantry Medal by Her Majesty the Queen. Hearing it then sent a shiver through me, as I remembered that moment in my cabin at Zeebrugge, just hours from the most horrendous night of my life.

I lay there listening to the music, reflecting on my life. I thought of my son Simon, and how his face was a joy to wake up to. I had married late in life, relatively speaking, and it seemed to me now that there was a real purpose for living as now I had responsibilities for those other than myself. For the first time there was some stability in my life. I felt very warm and very happy and grateful to be alive.

I had always found it hard to express my true feelings, to actually say the things out loud that I felt. It is difficult to simply say 'I love you' to someone; a father, perhaps, or a brother or a mother, and not just to your wife or girlfriend. As I lay there I vowed I would be more open to those I loved. I thought how nice it would be to have another child. Anne and I had talked about it, as we liked the idea and did not believe Simon should grow up as an only child. My parents were separated, and I thought of my father and how much I admired his courage in tackling life.

I suspected Charles and David might come up for a chat, but they didn't, so I read the *Today* newspaper, and relaxed to the music.

My reverie was disturbed by the crackle of the walkie-talkie. Foot passengers were being embarked. I got up, switched off the cassette, silencing Mozart, and went back to my post.

I made a Tannoy announcement for the benefit of my staff: 'Attention catering department and catering personnel, open all services. Passengers on board.'

Dave Disbury came up to the counter, we had a brief chat about meal breaks, and he said, 'I'll have a meal first, then come and relieve you.' I was never to see him again.

Andrew Parker passed by and said, 'Do you have any cabins?' It was already getting a bit rowdy as many passengers headed for the bar, and I think he and his family and friends wanted some peace and quiet on the return trip. But I had to disappoint him. Freight drivers are automatically given cabins, and I had to make sure they had received their allocation before I started offering any surplus to other passengers. I told Andrew, 'We may have, but you'll have to wait until we sail, and if there are any left I'll make an announcement.'

Paul White, the Chief Cook, came down to my

counter and we talked about obtaining some supplies. We could hardly hear each other over the noise of the passengers who were now on board.

I dialled the radio shack – 13 on the dial – to ask the Radio Operator to get in touch with another vessel and see that the necessary stores were left at Dover. There was no reply. I dialled again, but again there was no reply. The ship was still at berth stations as Steward Paul Cormack brought up the ship's bag, a soft container which holds the Captain's manifest of cargo, passengers and freight.

I remember two rows of people queuing at the bar, most of them *Sun* readers, quite a few of them clearly the worse for wear.

Sitting down I took the ship's bag and started working on the papers, the car and freight manifest. I had to pass these figures to Radio Operator Robert Mantle, who would then radio them to Dover. The aim was to tell the workers at the berth how many semi-trailers we had on board (that is the rear detached half of an articulated lorry), and how many tractors (the driving cab half of an artic) they would need to get them off.

We would radio also how many foot passengers we had on board, so that they could organise the requisite number of coaches and baggage trolleys, and if we had any animals on board that needed quarantine at Dover (there were no animals that day).

I dialled 13 again; still there was no reply from the radio shack. I replaced the receiver and made a mental note to try again in a few minutes. In fact I never did speak to Robert Mantle, and he died when the *Herald* went over.

I looked outside and could see it seemed very cold, a fact borne out by the faces of the passengers who had the keen red cheeks of those who have been out in low temperatures.

The ship moved. We were sailing. The nightmare was about to begin.

# 6

# *Escape and Rescue*

We sailed 20 minutes late because of delays in loading, but eventually we started to move out through the inner harbour. Paul White was still talking to me when my telephone rang. I answered it immediately, 'Information Office.'

It was John Butler, the freight drivers' Steward, and he was extremely agitated. He said, 'Steve, there's water coming down.'

'Where's it coming down?'

'It's coming down the stairs.' He sounded very nervous and excited.

On a ship you can get water coming in from different places, a toilet, a scupper, a burst pipe perhaps, and it is not rare. But any and every report of an unexplained source of water on board ship is serious and is given priority. And I could tell from John's voice that this was far more ominous than a burst pipe or overflowed toilet.

'OK John, I'll get the chippy [carpenter],' I said quickly. He would be the man to investigate such a leak. I put the telephone down. (John Butler survived.) I moved the five feet to the Tannoy system, pressed a switch, lifted the microphone and pressed the button on its side that allowed me to broadcast.

'Ship's Carpenter contact the Information Office immediately.' Then I repeated the message.

Much was said after the disaster to the effect that this was some sort of code. It was not. It was a clear and direct message that in the event proved irrelevant because of the speed and nature of what was happening.

The Carpenter Mick Tracey told me later he was in his cabin on F Deck when he heard the message. He got up from his chair to pick up the telephone and call me when the ship started to roll.

At the same time I felt the ship heel to port. I was not unduly alarmed, it was a steep roll, but ships have gone like that before when the Quartermaster makes a tight turn to avoid another ship which has foolishly cut across its bows.

The *Herald* righted itself, tilted a fraction to starboard, came back, and started to roll to port again. This time it did not come back. There next followed the scenes of horror I described earlier, and on which I have no wish to dwell.

After my escape and the incidents I described, I grabbed a sea axe from one of the ferry's lifeboats and started to smash at the one-inch thick glass of the massive porthole windows. Some people said later that broken glass fell on them as they huddled inside, but this could not have been avoided as we had to get lifelines through, and that was the only way to do it. In addition, breaking the glass – that physical barrier between the trapped people and the hull – was a tremendous psychological boost.

I saw one man in his sixties, who I later learned lost four generations of his family, working tirelessly to help get people out.

We desperately needed a ladder and I eventually got one from the crewman of a rescue tug which had nosed into the forward section of the *Herald*. It was aluminium, about 16 feet long, and not too heavy. I carried it back to the midships area near the cafeteria entrance on C Deck.

I secured it with a rope to cleats on the vessel, and lowered it through one of the smashed porthole windows.

I saw people coming up.

Stewardess Moyna Thompson was one, and she was visibly shaking all over. Over and over she was saying 'I can't believe it, I can't believe it'. Then she seemed to recover her composure and asked, 'What can I do to help?'

Once again I remembered the lesson I had learned from reading about the sinking of the *Lusitania*. Take command, be forceful, get people to do things, make them useful.

Moyna had somehow survived and escaped from the

crew Mess, and I could see was in no fit state to help on the hull, so I told her, 'Get on that tug, wrap up the survivors, give them hot drinks and keep them warm.'

As the minutes passed I felt stronger and stronger. I saw some lads, clearly day trippers, standing out on the hull. They were huddled in a group, dazed and motionless, staring in disbelief at what was going on around them. I shouted at them to come with me to where other crew members were pulling people out. I saw the Bosun Terry Ayling and Quartermaster Tom Wilson going up and down the hull to get equipment, toiling tirelessly, to help pull out the injured, and also rescuing the Master, Mate and Second Mate from the bridge. In their opinion the Second Mate Paul Morter was hysterical, and so had to be pulled out first, before the badly-injured Master and First Mate.

Terry needed more lights and Paul offered to get them from a tug. He did not return. This left Terry the most senior deck rating on board, and he took immediate control of the rescue. I make no judgement on Paul Morter's behaviour, as none of us can know beforehand how we will react in such circumstances.

I moved to another area where I found a pilot ladder – basically a rope ladder with wooden or metal steps – had been lowered into one of the broken porthole windows. There was very little light but I thought I detected movement, and I called out, 'Come on.' I lay flat on the tilted hull and could now see what was the bedraggled figure of a woman clutching the ladder. I did not know at that moment, but it was Jenny Leslie, a Stewardess from the Duty Free perfume shop who had herself saved a little boy when the ship capsized.

Again I remembered the lessons of the *Lusitania*. Take command. Shout. Exhort to action. I did, screaming at her to move, to climb the ladder. I even swore, anything to get her moving. Eventually she was in reach of my hand, and grabbed it as though it was a lifeline. But grasping it somehow made her think that she was safe, and in her confused state, she then let herself go from the ladder.

Normally it would be hard enough to hold the dead weight of a grown woman just by the grip of hands. But my hand was cold, hers was soaking wet, oily and freezing. I gripped as tight as I could, but I honestly thought I was going to drop her. Had I done so, she would have fallen some 15 feet back into the icy water. I doubt that she would have survived.

I looked around frantically, and saw a couple of people near me, and screamed to them for assistance. They did not hear me at first because of the rest of the noise, and I had to reach out with my free hand and grab someone by the leg, begging, 'Give me a hand, quick, quick!'

It seemed to me that I had held on to Jenny's hand for hours, and my arm felt as though it was being gradually wrenched out of its socket. Our grip was loosening, but I was absolutely determined not to let go. Somehow I held on, and with the help of two others, eventually I got Jenny out. She was a dreadful sight, soaked to the skin, smeared with oil, her eyes glazed with shock. She was shaking with cold and she had absolutely no idea what was going on around her, so we got her off the ship as soon as we could. In the weeks following the disaster, I went and knocked on Jenny's door to see how she was, and to my embarrassment her husband and two children thanked me for saving her life. It was a very moving moment, and a gesture that touched Anne and myself deeply.

After Jenny had got off the *Herald*, I saw Ken Hollingsbee and asked him what had happened. He did not know. I asked after Dave Disbury. Had he got out? Ken replied, 'I think he's out.' Sadly that was incorrect. A lot of people that night *thought* they saw people safe who in fact were dead. It was almost as though faces we wanted to see were superimposed on others. I knew that if we were to get more people out, someone had to be on the inside of the hull, and every second that passed lessened the chances of survival of those inside. I got a torch from somewhere and went down one of the pilot ladders into the ship. I climbed down carefully, rung by rung, the torch in one hand, my other arm wrapped around the ladder as it swayed and swung under the impetus of my body's descent.

I was back on C Deck, somewhere aft of the cafeteria, and as the beam of the torch pierced the pitch blackness, I could see chairs and tables tipped up, and people in the water.

Then a woman started to scream, an eerie scream that made the hairs of my body stand on end. She was perched up on some seats, out of the water.

I saw that other people were using bolted-in tables as stepping stones to move towards another rope ladder that hung nearby.

I noticed a diver in the water, a huge man of well over six feet tall. He was a heroic Belgian who performed miracles that night. I knew that our first priority was to get the screamer out, for the noise she made was soul destroying. It was clearly having a terrible mental effect on those around her struggling for their lives. The diver helped her across to the ladder, and when I grabbed her she was trembling with fear, and the lower half of her was wet through. I coaxed her all the way up the ladder, urging her, 'You've got to save yourself.' It was 12 feet to the top, and those at the head of the ladder were calling to her, 'Come on my girl, come on my girl.' At last we reached the top and willing hands pulled her out to safety.

I went back down again and suddenly it was quiet except for the lapping of the water. Now I estimated that there were between 30 and 35 people in the water. The diver was holding people's heads out of the water to stop them drowning.

There was an accumulation of dead people at the base of the ladder, and I could see that we were going to have to move them or haul them out before the living could get to the ladder. I got a rope around one woman who was clearly dead, and called on the rescuers above to haul her out. But when we pulled her from the water we discovered that she was tangled by a lifejacket to another body. I asked the diver for his knife and tried to cut her free. It seemed like an eternity but at last something parted, and the attached body fell back into the water with a splash.

With the sudden lessening of the burden, the weight eased on the rope-pullers, and the first woman shot upwards. Her face stopped within inches of mine. Her eyes were staring, the face empty of life and expression, and I shuddered.

Then in the water I saw Glen Butler, a Compactor Steward and a friend of mine, married with two kids. He had his lifejacket on, done up properly as per regulations, and he seemed very calm. I said, 'Hello Glen, you OK?' 'I'm fine, Steve, see to the passengers,' he answered. He could quite easily have forced his way over, climbed the ladder and got out. But he did not. He was crew and he felt that the passengers' safety came first.

I lost track of Glen as I bullied, coaxed and cajoled people up the ladder. Then I could not see him, and realised the current moving inside the ship must have pulled him away from where the ladder was. I had been joined on the ladder by a Seaman, Brian Kendall. I told him, 'I'm going after Glen.' I was worried about him being in the water all that time. But Brian talked me out of going after him, so I thought I would ask the diver to find Glen. How I wish now that I had not listened to Brian, although I know he was only concerned for my safety.

I passed ropes under the arms of some of those we

rescued, making a crude loop, and pleading with them to keep their arms tight to their sides as they were hauled up, so that the rope would not slide up and over their heads. But they had been in icy-cold water for too long, they were shocked, and the freezing immersion had made them lose feeling in their limbs. As they rose higher, I could see arms start to come up from their sides. Two people fell this way, slipping out of the loop. One man survived the fall, but the result of the drop and the second immersion was too much for one woman and despite the kiss of life, she died.

Nine or ten times I went down that ladder, and eventually the inevitable happened. I was holding someone up when my foot slipped and I fell into the water. It was bloody cold, and the shock of it took my breath away. But somehow I managed to hold on to my torch and keep it out of the water.

I saw one man in the water who had a big chunk of bone and flesh missing from the front of his head. But to my surprise instead of asking for help, he said, 'Are you all right mate?' I was stunned at his concern for *me*. But then something galvanised him, and he surged forward, pulled himself onto the ladder, climbed it and escaped.

Next I felt hands on me, pulling me down, as a couple of people clutched at me in panic. I thought, 'Oh no, I'm going to go under.' With an effort I struggled free and regained my footing on the ladder, hauling myself out of the water.

The next few hours are now a blur to me, and I

do not know if the events I describe happened in a chronological order. But I can remember distinctly that the people around me in the water made no cries, but the looks on their faces were pitiful, full of disappointment that they were still there in that black, freezing hell of a place, when others were safe.

I saw a man holding a baby by gripping his teeth on to its clothes, and someone managed to get a rope thrown down and the father tied the rope around the baby. At the sight of the tiny mite being hauled up I thought, 'How can something so small have survived this?' I was actually weeping tears of joy.

Then suddenly the rope jerked. The idiots were pulling too hard and too fast. The baby swung like the end of a pendulum, and to my horror its head smacked into the bulkhead with sickening force. I felt bile in my throat and sheer nausea. I was fiercely angry that some idiot had killed that baby through thoughtlessness when it had survived the worst part of that hell. I looked at the father and saw the shock and disbelief in his eyes. But amazingly the little beauty survived with nothing worse than severe bruising on its forehead.

One man had a caramel-coloured liquid bubbling out of his mouth and nose. The diver realised he was dead and pushed him gently away.

Suddenly I remembered Glen. I asked the diver to find him, not knowing that it was over four hours now since the capsize. The diver found him, but shook his head at me. Glen had died from hypothermia; the cold had killed him as he waited valiantly, patiently and dutifully while we rescued others.

I will regret to my dying day that I did not go in myself and try and bring Glen out early on, when I first thought of it. If I had, perhaps he would still be alive today. It haunts me even now as I write these words to think of him in the water in his lifejacket, saying, 'I'm fine, Steve, see to the passengers.'

Seeing him dead in the water shocked me to the core, and suddenly that was enough, I felt I could do no more. My strength had gone, and I felt totally drained mentally and physically. I came out.

I had been on the capsized *Herald* over five hours. One of the Townsend Thoresen Masters, Captain Malcolm Shakesby, who had come aboard with the rescuers, came over and said, 'How are you?'

All I could say was, 'It's terrible, terrible. Is anyone else alive?' Then, hardly believing my own words, I said, 'We've got to go back inside.' I was exhausted, and it would have been impossible, but some part of my mind was still thinking we could do more.

Malcolm told me, 'You've done enough.' He put a blanket around my soaked body and led me towards a rescue tug. But something in me was reluctant to leave the *Herald*. I felt that as long as I was there some hope remained for those still missing.

I have strange memories of the odd incongruous things that happened. The most startling are of the people we rescued: almost every one was clutching on to something, a handbag, or a newspaper, some item of personal possession. Many even held onto their Duty

Free bags full of sodden cartons of cigarettes or broken liquor bottles. What possible use could they have been, even if they were intact, and who would risk their lives for a bottle of cheap Scotch? But it seemed that people wanted to cling on to something that was their own, something that reminded them of normality.

At last Quartermaster Tom Wilson and I were put onto a tug, the last crew members to leave the *Herald*, and the small boat pulled away from our overturned ship. I watched it as we moved further and further away, seeing it for the first time in dramatic view, surrounded by rescue ships and bathed in light. All I could think was, 'We're going on re-fit on Monday.' But the *Herald* was going nowhere now for a very long time.

It took a while to get to Zeebrugge, and I sat in the small cabin, a blanket around me, drinking the most beautiful, comforting hot coffee I have ever tasted.

My mind was obsessed with the *Herald*. I was still wondering if there could be people on board trapped in pockets of air below decks? Heat sensors! We could use them to find trapped survivors. And on and on it went, my mind racing like an engine out of control. Perhaps I should have wept, but the truth was I was too exhausted even to cry.

The tears would come later.

# 7

# *Anne, It's Me, I'm OK*

We landed at a quayside back in Zeebrugge, climbing up the rusty metal handholds embedded in the damp concrete. Waiting to greet us were harbour officials who asked our name and rank, making a written note of them. They all spoke English and we realised there were some people there from the Townsend Thoresen Zeebrugge office.

Within seconds we were aboard waiting mini-bus ambulances, their blue lights flashing, and we were being asked by medical personnel if we had suffered any injury. The injured and the non-injured were separated, and put into different ambulances. Myself and three other uninjured males, all passengers, were put in the same vehicle which then sped off on the road to Bruges.

All along the route, cars had been hastily parked at the roadside, as locals flocked to the coast to see what they could of our stricken vessel. No doubt they had heard of the calamity on television and radio news bulletins, and some morbid curiosity had drawn them out of their homes on that cold March night.

To me they were ghouls. What could they hope to see? And what could they possibly wish to see? Drowned human beings? But they had flocked to the scene, as I understand humans do often to air and train crashes, drawn by God knows what impulse. Some even took their children and that left a very bitter taste in my mouth. Children were dying on that vessel, some of my best friends were missing on it, and these sick parents were turning the disaster into a spectacle for their own kids.

At one point on our journey we even hit a traffic jam caused by the sheer volume of cars going to the coast. When time is crucial with seriously ill people being rushed to hospital, the activities of those thoughtless spectators could have cost a life.

We stopped briefly at a clinic, got out, and a man in a white coat who was presumably a doctor, asked the four of us, 'Are you OK? Do you have any pains?'

We all said that we did not and that we were uninjured. Then we piled back into the ambulance and continued our journey. The blankets seemed to have incredible heat-retaining properties for I was warm very quickly and my clothes appeared to have dried on me. I was to learn later that my trousers hadn't.

As the ambulance hurtled through the night I did not shake and I did not cry; I seemed to be suspended in some void. There was no yesterday and no tomorrow. My mind was just locked on the *Herald* and her plight. I could think of nothing but the *Herald*.

I thought 'if only' this, and 'if only' that. Should we have used a boat hook to fish people out of the water? We kept boat hooks in the lifeboats. And if we had had safety harnesses, we could have saved more people. That way they could not have slipped out of the ropes we tied around them. (I would later make this point to the official inquiry.)

The other three men in the ambulance were talking, but I did not take their conversation in. I just kept thinking 'Who's survived?' The only people I could be absolutely sure of were those I had seen with my own eyes.

At last the ambulance reached a naval base at Bruges, and pulled up outside a block of flats. We all filed out and went indoors to a foyer where people buzzed busily around. We were taken upstairs into a dormitory with a small room off it, that contained a kitchenette and a TV. The TV had a dial-tuner and special adaptor allowing it to pick up 20 European stations, including the BBC in colour. The first image I saw was of the *Herald* on its side. I gasped. I felt I was part of that ship and that I should still be on her.

The British announcer said the roll-on, roll-off ferry had capsized with an estimated 600 people on board. We sat glued to the set. The voice said, 'Now we will return to normal viewing.' We watched the BBC until it finally closed down, when I realised suddenly I was bursting to go to the loo. The urinals stank, a couple were overflowing, and my instinctive thought was 'This should be cleaned up'. I had believed for a moment that

I was back on the *Herald*, and that we could not allow toilets in this condition. As I urinated gratefully I realised that I had not been to the loo since before the *Herald* actually left its berth.

At about 1-45 a.m. local time – an hour earlier in England – I realised that people were telephoning wives and relatives in England. And I knew that I had contacted no one – Anne, my family, *no one* – to tell them that I had survived. And that they must be out of their minds with worry if they had seen the news bulletins. The Belgians had supplied telephones, and I picked one up and direct-dialled my home. I shall let my wife Anne describe in *her* words, how she heard the news, and how she coped.

That Friday evening I went to my painting class. Steve's father was baby-sitting Simon, and I was looking forward to the evening. I left about 6-40 p.m. before the first news-flashes. I remember that Glen Butler's mother was also a pupil at the class, and was there that night.

Steve's Dad had not been watching TV, but Steve's brother Robin and his wife saw it on the news at their home in Hythe, and my sister-in-law came over in her car. I was at class, blissfully unaware of what was happening, as was Glen's mother. But when I got home at about 9-20, I saw my sister-in-law's car, and I knew immediately that something was wrong. My first thought, of course, was that it was Simon. I can remember thinking, 'My God, something's happened to

Simon'. The thought that Steve could be in trouble never entered my head.

I got in and asked immediately, 'Is Simon OK?' Then they told me about the *Herald*. I was shocked, but strangely I was not frightened. I am not religious, but I felt instinctively that Steve was OK. In fact I was *sure* of it.

The news bulletins gave a Kent police telephone number offering information to relatives. We tried it continually but got the engaged tone. Steve's father was terribly upset. Friends in America telephoned as they had seen the news on bulletins over there; Steve's brother Clifford called from Canada where he now lives. People even knocked on our door. And all we could say was 'We don't know.'

At length we got through to the Kent police, but they could not give us any positive information.

After midnight, in fact 30 minutes before Steve called, the police telephoned. They said Steve was on a list of survivors.

Then the telephone rang. A voice said, 'Anne. It's me, I'm OK. I can't speak too long, there's people waiting.'

I turned to everyone and said, 'It's Stephen, he's OK.' And we were all in tears . . .'

There was no time for romance or emotion when I talked to Anne. I think I was too shocked for that anyway. I was still in a mess. I cannot even remember the conversation, and after about a minute I said, 'I have to go now, there's someone else wants to telephone.'

There was food in the kitchenette, bread and slices of cold meat, but I did not eat. I just drifted in and out of conversations, and when the last news bulletin finished it was as though a link had been cut, an air supply gone.

I went outside into the cold night air to see where I was, but nothing gave me a clue, and there was no one around. I had this urge to get back to Zeebrugge, but nothing was stirring and so I went back inside.

I realised that I had not yet taken my damp trousers off, and now I did so, putting on a pale-blue pair of trousers and a short-sleeved shirt that some kind official had given me.

We put the lights off in the dormitory, but no one seemed to sleep. We just talked, voices in the darkness trying to gain comfort from one another. One man said, 'I've got four members of my family on board, and I don't know what's happened to them.'

I lay there thinking of Glen's parents, and what they would do when they knew. Who was going to tell them? I was glad that was not to be my job.

I did not feel sleepy at all. My body was physically shattered and craved rest, but my mind was racing and would not let me sleep.

It became light around 7 a.m., and we heard people walking about. We got up and had some coffee, then dressed. My original clothes were a little damp, especially the trousers, but I put them on all the same. To me it seemed important that I retain my identity.

We were driven to the Novotel, a modern hotel which was part of an international chain, situated on the outskirts of Bruges. We got there at about 10-30, to see hordes of press and TV crews from all the European countries including Holland, Belgium of course, France and Germany, as well as Great Britain. Later there would be crews from Italy, Spain and the United States. I was still waiting for someone to pinch me hard.

Inside the lobby I saw Jenny Leslie, the Stewardess I had managed to hold onto and help rescue. Tom Wilson arrived with me, along with Steward Johnny Jackson who had glass cuts to his head. I saw Moyna Thompson, the Senior Stewardess, who still looked shocked and dazed.

We lunched together, grouped like an exclusive club, huddling to each other for emotional support. We sipped at some soup and picked at pieces of chicken, but none of us really had any appetite. Some of us had a beer, one or two chose brandy.

A surviving passenger told me he had been eating with his wife in the *Herald*'s restaurant when the ship keeled over. He described seeing Stewardess Marie Richards cling to a cash till, then lose her grip and fall through the air. Marie died, and so did the passenger's wife.

The press and TV people were in the lobby now. Some were polite, others pestered, and one or two were downright rude, unpleasant and intrusive.

I sat at a table with five of the crew survivors. Tom Wilson told me how he had helped rescue the Master, David Lewry, and the First and Second Mates. As he spoke the lobby doors opened, someone came in, and there was an almighty rush as the reporters, photographers and TV cameramen swooped. It was two members of the Belgian royal family, who had come to visit survivors. Officials directed them towards the five of us at our table.

But as they came over, it was like a small crowd moving towards us, surrounded as they were by the media who hung on their every utterance. When they reached us I felt terribly claustrophobic. Crown Prince Bernhard was trying to talk to us, but there was a lot of noise, with photographers shouting 'Look this way', 'Over here', 'Move to one side'. We were surrounded by a group of people, and one photographer even climbed up on a window ledge behind me so he could shoot through towards the Belgian royals. He kept pushing my head to one side because my head was in the way of his shot, saying, 'Can you move mate?' With the sound of the camera motor-drives, and the questions, it was actually hard to hear what Prince Bernhard was saying. It was not just the British media either, as, if anything the foreign press and TV were worse; they just did not seem to care about us at all.

Later when the royals had gone and the fuss had died down, everything was fairly calm in the lobby. Then a solitary middle-aged man walked in through the Novotel doors. He went across the lobby, sat down on the floor, put his head in his hands, bowed his whole body and began to weep. It was no ordinary weeping. He sobbed and sobbed, his body convulsed. It was an open and unashamed grief, the like of which I have never seen before nor wish to see again. He must have lost someone very dear to him, although I never learned who he was or the circumstances of his grief.

Seeing that sorrow was bad enough. But in seconds of his being overcome, the press pounced. They literally jumped up from wherever they were sitting, and converged on him like an angry swarm of bees. They fired questions at him. Who was he? Had he been on the *Herald*? Had he lost a relative? And as the reporters asked their questions the photographers took shot after shot of his abject misery. So keen was one photographer, that he even got down on the floor, stretched full out, right up close to the weeping man, and tried to point his camera up through the man's arms to record the agony of that face buried in hands that were trying to shut out the world.

Thankfully the man was oblivious to it all. He was alone, isolated by a misery that could not be comprehended by those who clustered around him. At last the photographers were satisfied and everyone fell back, the reporters getting no response to their urgent questions.

Those survivors who witnessed the scene were very, very angry. We knew the media had a job to do, but viewing its actions at close quarters as we had, made us doubt their sensitivity and judgement. It was not an edifying spectacle.

# 8

# *Windows of the Soul*

The question could not be avoided. Who was to identify the bodies?

As a new parent myself I hoped that if, God forbid, I was ever in the position of losing a child, someone would spare me that dreadful task of identification. I told John Kirby, the senior *Herald* Master, who was assisting us in Belgium, that I would identify what bodies I could to save a wife or parent having to do it.

He said, 'OK Steve, I'll have to see the necessary officials.' Tom Wilson said he would accompany me when we finally got permission to visit the temporary mortuary.

First, we gave statements to the Belgian police. During the interviews, the officers, some of whom did not have a full grasp of English, were constantly interrupted; owing to this and the language barrier, the statements were fragmented, terse, and did not seem to serve any useful purpose. But to be fair, the uniformed police officers who took down the statements were polite and courteous, and the task was soon over.

Townsend Thoresen staff were trying to get what crew they could out on the next available ferry, and two National Union of Seamen officials, Colin Bennett and George Higgins, had arrived in Belgium to add their efforts to the welfare work.

We were taken to a good-class restaurant on the seafront at Zeebrugge, which in other times and in the right mood would have been very pleasant. Next door to it was a clothes shop, and the union officials were giving the crew money to kit themselves out again. I hardly felt like eating, and half-heartedly ordered a crab dish as a starter. It seemed wrong to even *think* of eating under the circumstances. Everyone was talking feverishly about what had happened, and I can remember looking at those familiar faces and seeing them in a totally different way. They were shocked and disbelieving. They had come close to dying in a most awful way, and their faces and expressions showed it. They had lost friends, colleagues, and the grief shone from their eyes.

My food arrived and I took a reluctant mouthful as John Kirby walked in. He said, 'Are you ready Steve?'

We drove off, first to the Town Hall, trying to get the necessary permission to visit the mortuary. But when we got back to the dock area around 6-30 that evening, we were still without the official go-ahead we had to have.

We were shown into some offices, and I could see a

member of the local Marine Department drawing a diagram of how they planned to raise the *Herald*. It had a morbid fascination for me. I had been thinking all day of how exactly they could go about it. We moved on to the Port Authority offices where decisions were at the moment being taken about which company would be given the job of trying to lift the *Herald* from the sandbank on which she lay.

Tom and I were introduced to a man named Christopher Kenyon, who I understand is an expert pathologist and someone who specialises particularly in identifying bodies destroyed beyond normal recognition. He had worked on corpses recovered from the crash of an Air India Boeing 747 destroyed by a bomb over the Atlantic in 1975. No doubt he was in Zeebrugge to do post-mortem examinations on *Herald* victims.

Kenyon was accustomed to violent and shocking death, and dealing with the gruesome aftermath. He was calm and businesslike; we were calm through shock and cold, in spite of the task we faced. He talked to us quietly about the job of identifying corpses, and told us that bodies had been buried before under wrong names because those given the task of identifying them had been hasty and made mistakes. When the errors were finally discovered, the bodies had had to be disinterred and reburied, which had caused inestimable grief and emotional upset to the relatives. Kenyon stressed that we must not rush. We should take a good, long look and be absolutely sure before we made our decision.

We did not have to be told that the bodies in the mortuary were not long-dead ones. There would not be the extra horror of the effects of sea water and natural deterioration. But we were warned that faces have different expressions in death. Some are peaceful, and some are not. Kenyon said to us, and these words will always remain with me, 'When their eyes are open you are looking into the window of their soul.'

It would not be long before I understood exactly what he meant.

There were more telephone calls and at last we got back into the car and went off to a police sub-station. This time we found the local coroner, who was the right man to give us the permission we needed.

It was midnight on Saturday, 7 March, when we finally pulled up outside what appeared like a Boy Scout hall or a youth club where teenagers might play table tennis and listen to pop records.

I had now been awake for 40 hours.

We were allowed in after presenting our permissions, and a curtain of flag material screened the lobby area from the rest of the hall. I will never forget what I saw. Five rows of bodies, totalling 57, some in coffins, some in zip-up bags, were lying on the linoleum floor. A team of boys and girls, who seemed to be no older than 16, dressed in Red Cross uniforms, were tending to the dead. Kneeling on the floor, they reached into the coffins and the bags, gently washing faces. At the foot of each body they placed a tiny, fragile posy of flowers. There were no priests and no nuns, just these khaki-clad youngsters, moving quietly and lovingly among the dead.

A plain-clothed official approached and took us to the first line. The first body was not lying flat in the coffin, as for some reason the head and shoulders were propped up.

My mind went back to my days as a choirboy when we got 3s. 6d. ($17\frac{1}{2}$ pence) for singing at a funeral. The other lads used to tease me that one day a body would pop out of the coffin. As I sang I used to keep half-an-eye fearfully on the coffin.

Now here was the reality, a man aged between 45 and 50. He had one eye partially open. My first thought was, 'He paid £1 for this on the *Sun* day trip. And he ends up in a coffin.' He was no one I knew, and Tom and I moved on to the next.

This was Glen Butler, my friend. I had seen him drift slowly away to his death. He had refused to jump the queue for survival. I knelt down beside the coffin and it was as though Glen was asleep in bed. He looked at peace with the world, totally at peace. I had used to worry badly about death, but after that moment I knew it would worry me no longer. A sense of calm enveloped me. I felt instinctively then that some part of you goes on. Glen was totally unmarked, and he really looked as though he was asleep, his eyes tightly closed.

We moved on to the next body. It was Clayton Dyer, a Steward on the *Herald*. Clayton and Glen had been very close in life, and it seemed fitting that they should now be close in death. Clayton's eyes were open, and the pathologist's words came back to me . . . 'a window on their soul'. It seemed so true. It was like looking into a deep tunnel into a person's very soul. I moved on, only later wishing that I had closed Clayton's eyes.

The bodies had been laid out with men in the first two rows, women and children in the later rows. At each body I looked, I was unconsciously making some justification or rationale for their death, like 'Well, he's sixtyish, at least he's seen something of life.' I also had an incredible curiosity about the lives of those who had died. Has he got kids? Is he a baker or an accountant? What kind of life has she lived?

There was no displeasing smell or distinctive odour of death, but a few of the faces were contorted, the teeth bared in a final grimace.

The men and women were mostly middle-aged or elderly, but then I came to the children. Now I saw pathetically small coffins and a tiny body in a bag. Then the true enormity of the disaster hit me. I imagined if it was my son Simon down there. How could I do it? *Could* I do it? Identify the body of my own son?

I knew then that I would want someone to blame for this. I would want vengeance. At that moment it was the only natural reaction.

Walking between each coffin was only a matter of a few feet, but it seemed like an enormous distance, and the more I walked the harder it became.

When it was over, only then did tears well up in my eyes. I looked back and saw those young Red Cross boys and girls ministering to the dead. I thought of that baby, and how tiny it was. It had barely been alive, and would never know the joy of growing up. And I thought of eyes open. Windows on the soul.

The first evidence of the uncaring, even callous attitude of the Townsend Thoresen management – and later P & O, when that company took over Townsend Thoresen –, appeared less than 48 hours after the disaster.

Surviving passengers were flown back to England. Some of the crew asked to return home by hydrofoil from Ostend. Townsend Thoresen refused, saying the crew must leave by ferry from Zeebrugge. This meant, of course, that they would sail past the stricken hulk of the ship on which they had very nearly lost their lives, and which still contained many unrecovered bodies, some of them likely to be friends and colleagues. There was a distinct lack of compassion in that decision.

John Kirby booked me a room in the Novotel, as I did not wish to return to England just then. He also found me a jacket, a bright orange Townsend Thoresen anorak. I had been in my shirt sleeves and it was cold.

The man in the cafeteria at the Novotel looked as though he had had a bellyful of the whole circus. He must have been working non-stop coping with officials, survivors and media people. But despite the early hour when Tom Wilson and I returned, he rustled up steak and chips for us both, and we got ourselves some lager.

Over in the bar we noticed Townsend Thoresen's Liaison Officer Reg Hallett sitting with the Second Mate,

Paul Morter. Each had a drink in hand as Tom and I joined them. I knew how Paul had reacted to the disaster but I did not hold it against him. As I've written, none of us can truly predict how we will react in such a situation. But Paul's next actions were less easily forgiven. When Tom went off to the loo, Paul suddenly said, 'Do you think Tom will panic?'

I asked Paul what he meant, and he replied, 'You know, under pressure.' I presumed he meant at the inevitable inquiry. I gritted my teeth and said, 'Of course he won't panic.' I was bitterly angry.

We had another beer each, and I could still feel anger and adrenalin pumping through me. We were booked on a 7-30 a.m. hydrofoil from Ostend – we had been allowed that – and had to get up at 5-45. It was 3-15 when at last I slumped onto my bed, waiting for the alarm call I had booked for two and a half hours later. I slept a little, but fitfully, with images rather than dreams punctuating my slumber.

A cab took us to Ostend, and surprisingly, there were no feelings of fear or trepidation as we stepped on to the hydrofoil. This was probably because it seemed more like a plane than a ship. The 'pilot', which is how a hydrofoil Captain is described, came down and made us welcome. He invited us up to the bridge, and at first he obviously did not want to broach the subject. But being a Master himself, he could not resist it, and asked us a few questions which we answered.

As we approached Dover it seemed uncannily quiet, and a lifetime since that Friday morning, which was only less than 48 hours before, when the *Herald* had nosed her way out of the harbour and into the English Channel.

We had to go through immigration control, and a policeman was waiting to make a note of our age, birthdate and address, presumably to check those off against their list of survivors.

The hydrofoil came in at Western Docks, not the Eastern, where most of the press were waiting for survivors, and so we escaped attention. A company minibus was waiting to take us home, and as Tom lives at Deal, we agreed he could be dropped off first.

En route I wanted to see David Disbury's family. I had everything planned, all the proper things I should say, and yet all I wanted to give them was good news. Yet I could not do that because I had none. David was still missing. His sister answered the door. His wife, who had two small children, was still in shock. Once again the awfulness of it all hit me, and the planned words were useless. Tears welled up and I was gone. At the doorstep David's sister kissed me on the cheek and said simply, 'Thank you.'

On the way to Tom's house we stopped at a newsagent and bought every newspaper we could lay our hands on, reading the different stories avidly. Seeing the picture of the *Herald* on its side, bow doors gaping open, I recalled Mark Stanley's chilling words, 'I left the doors open.'

Now they made horrific sense. Tom and I talked, going over it all again, and I am sure the driver could

Stephen, Anne and Simon.

*Top. Herald of Free Enterprise* at sea.

*Bottom.* The *Herald's* sister ship *Pride of Free Enterprise* in dry dock with her bow doors open. This picture shows how close the bottom of the bow doors are to the sealine in ro-ro ferries.

*Top.* The first articulated lorry is salvaged from the capsized ferry.

*Bottom.* The open bow doors, through which the seawater flooded the vehicle deck of the *Herald*, can clearly be seen.

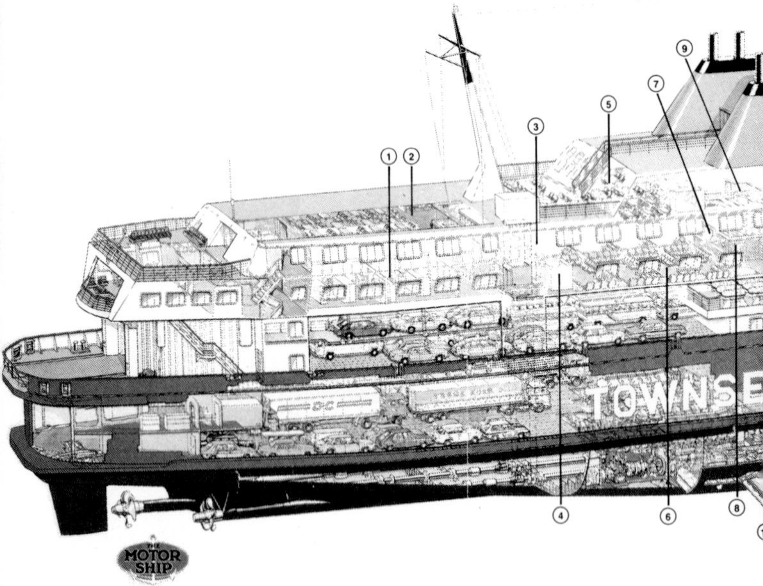


Reproduced with permission

(1) DUTY FREE SHOP C DECK
(2) BAR B DECK
(3) MAIN BAR AREA C DECK
(4) PERFUME SHOP C DECK
(5) RESTAURANT AREA B DECK
(6) WHERE STEPHEN WENT BACK INTO SHIP C DECK
(7) INFORMATION OFFICE
(8) EXIT DOOR TO INFORMATION OFFICE
(9) SALAD BOWL B DECK
(10) LADIES TOILETS
(11) ALLEYWAY WHICH BECAME A DEATH CHUTE
(12) DOORS TO STEPHEN'S ESCAPE
(13) CAFETERIA AREA C DECK
(14) LIFE BOATS WHERE AXES AND TORCHES CAME FROM
(15) AREA JOHN BUTLER GAVE ALARM
(16) BRIDGE DOOR
(17) CAR DECK WHERE WATER FLOODED IN
(18) BOW DOOR

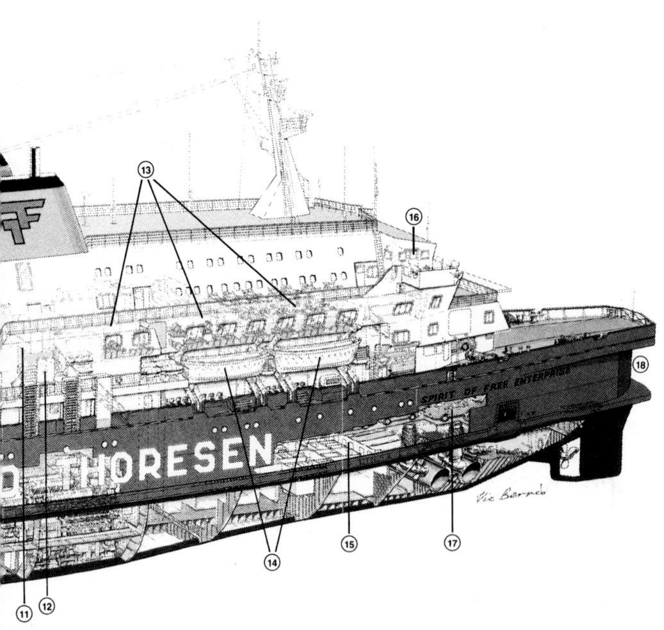


'SPIRIT OF FREE ENTERPRISE'
TOWNSEND THORESEN *Passenger & Vehicle Ferry*
*Drawn for 'Motor Ship' by Vic Berris FSIAD 1980*

**STEPHEN'S ESCAPE ROUTE IS SHOWN ON A PLAN OF THE *SPIRIT OF FREE ENTERPRISE*, THE *HERALD'S* IDENTICAL SISTER SHIP.**

*Top left.* David Didsbury. *Top right.* Glen Butler.

*Bottom.* Stephen (right) and Terry Ayling struggle to prevent the floral cross splitting in two at the televised memorial service.

*Top left.* Stephen and Malcolm Shakesbury, who helped co-ordinate the rescue procedure, collect their bravery awards at Buckingham Palace in March 1988.

*Top right.* 'Human bridge' Andrew Parker (left) displays his George Medal alongside Stephen.

*Bottom.* Anne congratulates Stephen on the Silver Life-Saving medal of the Order of St. John.

Survivors of the crew of
the *Herald of Free Enterprise*
aboard the *Vortigern*.

not understand the mattter-of-fact way we talked. But we had rehashed every aspect constantly.

Tom and his wife had an emotional reunion, and I quickly took the opportunity to telephone Anne. I said 'I'm back', and I could register the shock in her voice when she spoke to me.

When the driver finally dropped me off I could hear the birds singing. I swear that they seemed sweeter than ever before, that their song was more beautiful than I could recall. I was alive, and I was home.

# 9

# *Home*

My reunion with Anne and Simon was not one of tears or great displays of emotion. But it was a marvellous moment; we all hugged and kissed, and then there was my family to greet. Generally it was low key though. There was a tremendous amount of pent-up emotion within me, and although some of it would come out later in bouts of weeping, regrettably I bottled most of it up initially. Grief, sadness, and anger over what had happened churned around inside me. And in time this would lead to stress, anxiety and a brush with severe psychological illness.

But for now it was just enough that I was alive and reunited with my family. This tragedy had brought it home to me just how much I valued life with Anne and Simon, how dear to me was our life together, our home, our garden, the possessions we had acquired together.

It had made me realise too how trivial are most of our worries, and the great state we get ourselves into over events which have no major significance whatsoever.

My dear father said to me, 'I knew you'd go back inside.' Anne had had total faith too that I would return. How lucky I was to have them.

I could not relax and I could not lie down. I wanted to read newspaper accounts of the disaster, listen to news bulletins about rescues or survivors.

The shock had been like an anaesthetic, numbing my own emotion. As the shock wore off, so the grief, like pain, came flooding back. I suddenly broke down, weeping. I was exactly like the man sobbing in the Novotel, racked with weeping, shoulders heaving. I told those dear to me what I had never said, as it were publicly, before. I told Anne, Simon and my father how much I loved them. It was a cathartic moment for me. As I have said, I have always found it difficult to express emotion, but now I could.

Later there was a telephone call from Townsend Thoresen asking me to go to Enterprise House in Dover. They were trying to see if there was any chance at all that anyone could still be alive on the *Herald*, trapped in air pockets in the cabin areas.

There were TV crews in the main foyer when I arrived in the early evening, and I went straight up to the second floor, where an official from the Marine Department had plans of the ship opened on a board. He asked me questions about the drivers' cabins, and anything else that I could possibly add, such as areas of the ship I thought had the potentiality for air pockets and where passengers or crew might still be trapped.

I helped as much as I could, then came home wearily. I was now totally exhausted, but my mind still raced. Eventually something would have to give, I knew. There would be a point when my body would simply put itself to sleep. When I climbed into bed it happened. I remember nothing except waking up the next morning with Simon crawling over me.

The rest of the week passed in a blur of telephone calls, enquiries from well-wishers, and in the physical work of the decorating which Anne and I started. I did not want to mope about the house, and Anne did not want that either. The work had to be done, we had planned to do it, and so why not? In the event it was the best thing I could have done. The thought required to decorate made my mind concentrate on something other than the tragedy; and the sheer physical work, the lifting, the climbing ladders, the wielding of a paste brush, seemed to act as a soothing balm on me.

There was a telephone call of commiseration from my local Member of Parliament, Michael Howard. The Kent police called as well. On Monday morning a letter from Townsend Thoresen arrived. It was word-processed and it began, 'Dear   '. Really. Where my name should have been, there was a blank. It had been correctly addressed to me on the envelope, but either Townsend Thoresen had forgotten to insert the name, or else they were terrified that the letter might be arriving at the house of someone who was actually dead or missing.

They did not seem to trust their own records. It was a preformatted letter sent to all surviving crew. There were only 42 of us, and I do not think it should have been beyond Townsend Thoresen's capabilities to send each one of us an individual letter, instead of writing one with a blank for our names. A blank which in my case they had not filled in. The letter read:

> 'We do realise that there is little that can be said to minimise the terrible experience that you have suffered.
>
> If there is any way in which you feel the company can possibly be of assistance to you at this time, please do not hesitate to contact us immediately.'

There followed a list of telephone numbers for me to ring if I needed help. The letter continued:

> 'We will be in touch with you from time to time, but you should consider yourself on leave for at least the next two weeks.'
>
> It was signed J. J. Briggs, Managing Director.

I kept working away at the decorating, losing myself in the work. It stopped me sitting and thinking of Zeebrugge.

One night there was a knock on the door, and a young man stood nervously, shifting from foot to foot, a motor-cycle crash helmet in one hand. His name was Graham Anderson, and he was a reporter on our local newspaper, the *Folkestone Herald*. He had come on his motorbike, and it was clear this was his first big story.

He was not hardened to this kind of thing by experience, as some of the other reporters I had spoken to were. I asked him in and gave him coffee. He refused a brandy I think he badly needed.

I had barely given any interviews. I had simply not wanted to talk about it, and as I have said, the behaviour of some of the press and TV crews upset me badly.

But this was the local paper, and the local people needed to know what had happened; it was a local tragedy. And Graham seemed a very nice guy. It was his sheer innocence and lack of guile that made me talk to him. And as we spoke it became clear that the tragedy had touched him in a personal way too. He knew someone who had died on the *Herald*.

For the next days I was still in a daze, although I was not fully aware of it, though I suppose that *is* the definition of being in a daze. I would put two tea bags into one cup, instead of putting one in each cup. I would put cold water instead of hot into the teapot. Anne was very patient with me. I did not want to go out. I could not face the cinema or a restaurant. I just scraped at some old wallpaper with a frenetic energy.

I was still keeping in close touch with events in Zeebrugge, speaking by telephone with Richard Toptalo, an Assistant Purser from a different watch of the *Herald*. Richard had volunteered to go to Belgium and help in the welfare office, dealing with relatives, booking them into hotels and helping them all he could. He kept me up to date with the latest developments, and I was grateful for that link, rather than having to get my news from newspapers and TV.

On 11 March, there was another letter from J. J. Briggs:

> 'I want to say how sorry I was to hear of your appalling ordeal on board the *Herald of Free Enterprise*, and would like to wish you a full and complete recovery . . .'

Then someone brought round an envelope from Townsend Thoresen. I opened it and pulled out a cheque for £1,000. At the time I was furious as I felt the timing was appalling. We had risked our lives, our friends had died, at least in part because of the failure of the company to respond to requests for bow door safety measures, and now they were handing us £1,000 as though somehow the money could make it all better.

But when my anger subsided I realised that I had been over-hasty. The money was not vital to me and Anne, but for people in different circumstances – widows with immediate bills to pay, for example – it could have helped to alleviate real hardship, and so it was a thoughtful gesture on behalf of Townsend Thoresen. One of their few thoughtful gestures, I have to say.

At the time of writing, August 1988, with the exception of my severance pay when I left on medical grounds, that is the only money that I have received from Townsend Thoresen, or P & O who eventually took over the company. I understand too that the sum of £1,000 will be deducted from any compensation made to me. I and others are suing P & O for damages over the disaster. In my case I am suing for loss of my livelihood, as the Shipping Federation who control seamens' 'tickets', have declared me medically unfit for further service at sea.

By a strange quirk, on the same day that I received my money from Townsend, I received another cheque for £1,000 through the post. It was money left to me in the will of my grandmother who had died in January of that year.

Death had brought me £2,000 in one day, and never had money been less welcome.

The company held a debriefing for crew survivors, and I was asked by Alan Rutherford, one of the Masters, about my escape from the Information Office. At one point he asked, 'Did you go in the lifejacket locker and get the lifejackets out?'

I was so astonished at the naivety of this question, that I could only say, 'No.'

He looked at me then with a kind of stern reproving look, as though I should be ashamed of myself. Had he no understanding of what was involved? The key for the lifejacket locker is kept hanging up on a hook on a little grip, a kind of push-in clip behind the partition in the office itself.

The ship had just capsized at an angle of 90 degrees, it was pitch black and water was rushing in. As far as anyone knew we were sinking. I had escaped only by clinging to that very partition. To get the key to the lifejacket locker would have involved me searching in the dark for a tiny object. But worse, I would have had to lower myself into the part of the office that had become, by virtue of the capsize, a deep well.

It would have required the skill of a contortionist, and an ability to find the proverbial needle in the haystack. But let us say that I *had* managed to perform that feat. Again, because of the angle the ship was now listing, the lifejacket locker was a full nine feet above me. And had I achieved all that, what precisely would I have done with the lifejackets?

In fact, the water inside the ship did become full of lifejackets. And they got in people's way, they were a damn nuisance, there were more of them than was necessary. Yet this man, in the calm and orderly – and safe – atmosphere of an office, was mentally upbraiding me for not having opened the lifejacket locker. It was madness. He clearly had no imagination, or no comprehension of what it was like on the *Herald of Free Enterprise* in those terrifying minutes immediately following the capsize. I felt he was insulting both my courage and my efficiency, and I resented it strongly.

On 13 March the company's solicitors started to take statements from the crew. They overlooked asking me, but I learned about what was going on and volunteered to give a statement. Eventually I dictated my account to their lawyers at Channel House in Dover, I could not help noting that it was Friday the thirteenth. After I had signed the statement, I realised they had got the date of the tragedy wrong. They had put 6 *May* 1987, instead of 6 *March* 1987. It was such an elementary mistake, but it was an insulting one for those of us for whom the date would be engraved for ever on our memories. The slipshod attitude seemed to say, 'March, May – what does it matter? We all know when it happened.'

And that attitude of the company and its representatives pervaded everything from then on. They acted as if they wished the whole thing would go away. Zeebrugge was an embarrassment to them, particularly as damaging revelations began to seep out.

And if the tragedy was an embarrassment, what about the crew? We were the living, breathing, *talking* reminders of that night, and we would not go away. They could tow away the *Herald*, rename it and pack it off to Taiwan for scrap. But they could not do that to us, although sometimes I believe if there was some human scrap-heap, they would have consigned us to it if at all possible.

As I write this book it is 18 months since the *Herald* went over, and only two of the crew who survived that night are still with P & O. The company has wiped its slate clean.

# 10

## *For Those in Peril on the Sea*

Funerals and hymns, coffins and widows. The haunting verses of that hymn to sailors, 'Eternal Father strong to save, whose arm hath bound the restless wave.'

It seemed as though the burial services would never end, there were so many of them. And some perverse part of me did not want them to. This was because the funerals were the last link with my dead comrades and friends like David Disbury and Glen Butler.

Firstly there was a memorial service, a local one at the Parish Church of St Mary the Virgin, Dover. I did not wish to wear a uniform for the service, as it was held on the 14 March, so close to the event, and I did not want my uniform to be a constant reminder to the widows of their loss.

Anne and I left Simon with his grandparents and drove to Dover on a cold, dry day. I felt very emotional, my heart was pounding and I could feel adrenalin racing through me. I knew I would be meeting some of the widows for the first time, and by the time I got to the church my hands were clammy with the sweat of nerves.

Anne and I were in church half an hour before the start of the service, and we took seats at the front. The organ played mournful music at a low tempo, and there was a sense of growing gravity and awe as the church slowly filled. Before the start I passed a few words with Stewardess Gail Cook and her husband. Crazily we entertained hopes, wild hopes, that someone might still be lying unrecognised in a hospital somewhere. Yet deep within us I suppose we recognised them for the false hopes they were.

The service started, and we sang the first hymn: 'Immortal, invisible, God only wise. In light inaccessible, hid from our eyes.' Then that most British and comforting of hymns that seems to affect even the most cynical: 'Abide with Me. Fast falls the Eventide.'

The words of the hymns, the sound of those anguished voices raised in song, unleashed my own grief. I wept.

The Bishop of Dover gave his address, and though I can remember little now of what he said, I know the words were comforting to us all. Next came the hymn we were to hear so often:

'Eternal father strong to save,
Whose arm hath bound the restless wave.
Who bids the mighty ocean deep, its own appointed limits keep.
Oh hear us when we cry to Thee,
For those in peril on the sea.'

I was still in tears, and behind me several people were crying unashamedly too, as Anne comforted me. We all had something in common in that church, a shared grief, a bond of sorrow that united us all. I wept those familiar deep sobs, until my whole body ached. It gave me some momentary relief, but I knew then that my grief was deeper-rooted and more profound than I had realised previously.

This was partly because however much one wept, whatever kind words were said or hymns sung, the hard and inescapable truth was that the tragedy had happened; nothing could change that fact or bring back those who had perished.

Anne and I slipped out of church quickly when the service ended. There was enough grief there, and there was nothing any of us could say that could possibly make things easier for those who had been bereaved.

Some of the survivors and wives went for a drink at a nearby pub. We wanted something to deaden the pain, something to take the edge off the rawness we felt. Over the drinks I saw people I had not seen since the night of the 6th. We seemed to be closer than ever, a kind of brotherhood of shared experience, and no one who had not been there that night could possibly hope to penetrate that mysterious something that bound us to each other. I had three pints of beer and the alcohol seemed to act as a mild palliative, dulling the pain to some extent.

Anne drove us home, and we picked up Simon on the way. Back home I undressed to take a bath, because despite the cold weather I was sweating heavily.

In all I was a mourner at 24 funerals. Once I went to *five* in one day. And to me each one had its own personal significance.

The first was on 16 March, and was for Clayton Dyer, the man I had identified in the temporary mortuary at Zeebrugge; the man into whose 'windows of the soul' I had gazed.

The service at Barham in Kent, was packed. All the able-bodied crew survivors were present. Each of us felt it was important that the funerals be attended. I looked at the coffin, and my feelings were overwhelmingly strong. I *knew* the man inside, I had seen him dead in the mortuary, eyes open. I had identified him and shared that very final moment with him.

There was the familiar sad organ music, the hymns, and the 23rd Psalm 'The Lord Is My Shepherd I Shall Not Want'. And inevitably, 'Eternal Father Strong to Save'. We filed out to see hundreds of wreaths and bouquets of brightly coloured flowers. All the messages were so personal and there was so much love in them.

The C Watch on the *Herald* had been very close. We liked each other very much, we were happy working together, and got on well. Now, those feelings of love – and I do mean love – between fellow workmates, men to men, men to women, women to women, workmates to workmates, were shining through. They are feelings that most of us refuse to believe we have. They have nothing to do with sex or attraction, but rather the love of fellow human beings for one another.

And those feelings came out that day, as a spring of emotion. I went over to pay my respects to Clayton's father. He clasped his hands in mine, and said, 'Thanks for coming.' I realised that he was trying to make *me* feel comfortable, and my heart went out to him.

The emotion of the funerals, and the sheer strain of attending them, never altered. Each one was a deeply moving ordeal for all concerned. I suppose, though, it was only natural that as the funerals went on the number of mourners dwindled. But I could not help but notice that the higher the rank of the dead crew member, the better Townsend Thoresen were represented. It made me feel that rank and class distinction in life was being carried over, even into death, and this displeased me greatly.

Some of the Masters and senior officers clearly could not go because they had ships to take to sea, but I felt that shore-based management should have made it their business to see that each funeral was equally well-represented as far as Townsend Thoresen was concerned.

Ted Oldfield, a Steward who had served on the *Canberra* when it went down to the Falklands in 1982, was cremated after a service in Southampton. Only one crew member from the *Herald* could go, and it was reported that not a single member of P & O, the owners of the *Canberra* and who were later to take over Townsend Thoresen, was present. Ted's ashes were brought back to Dover and scattered at sea.

There was an interlude in the round of funerals. On Tuesday, 17 March, a Department of Trade Inspector, one Captain Miller, interviewed me in Dover. I was not very happy with the way he took my statement, and it did not appear to be a very thorough interview.

I had imagined that officials would want to know in detail what might help in any such future accident, and what equipment and procedures could perhaps minimise the extent of such a catastrophe. But this was not the case, and I was baffled. I would have imagined that the Department of Trade would have set up an expert team to carry out an exhaustive debriefing, learning lessons and gaining valuable experience for the future. In the end what I said ended up as a brief three-page statement of about 400 words.

The next funeral was Glen Butler's at Hawkinge Crematorium on a cold day. At the service they played records that had great sentimental value to Glen's parents.

Glen's mother had been with Anne at their painting class on the evening of the tragedy, both blissfully unaware of the accident until they returned home. And I had survived, and Glen had died.

I kept my composure during this funeral, as I seemed to have gained more control by then. Yet I could not shake off the awful knowledge that none of us need be here if I had gone into the water when I wished to, and rescued Glen. Or was I fooling myself? Would he have died anyway, or would we both perhaps have died? If I had any satisfaction at all that day it was in the knowledge that a passenger was almost certainly alive because Glen had chosen to stay in the water.

Well before Zeebrugge, Anne and I had booked tickets for the West End stage show of the TV French Resistance comedy *'Allo, 'Allo*. The tickets had been booked for that night, the night of the 8th, Glen's funeral. We decided to go anyway; perhaps it sounds callous, I don't know. I think those who have been in a similar situation will understand. It was not that we wanted to see a comedy. We just wanted to get away, to do something other than sit and think about Zeebrugge. We wanted to see bright lights, hear music, see colour and life after the awful solemnity and drabness of the many funerals.

But despite everything my mind kept going back to Glen's funeral. I knew there were to be many more.

Anne and I had a meal and a bottle of wine in a restaurant near the Prince of Wales theatre where the comedy was showing. The wine soothed me a little, and we took our seats, feeling better.

The show was funny and inconsequential, but I found I could not keep my mind on it. My concentration was totally gone, and I simply was not 100 percent there. Suddenly I would be aware that the whole audience was laughing, and I did not know why. I had missed some running gag, and the punchline.

Coming home on the train Anne and I did not talk much. I knew that I was becoming very short-tempered and irritable at home. Life seemed very bleak.

At the funeral of Senior Purser Brian Eades, in whose cabin I had spent some of his last hours, there was a break from the normal hymns with the music from the 'Skye Boat Song' – 'sail bonny boat like ... a bird on the wing, over the sea to Skye.' But, inevitably, there was 'Eternal Father strong to save...'

Brian had been a Freemason, and a senior member of that society came to the funeral, complete with bowler hat and neatly rolled umbrella.

At most of the funerals if there were TV crews present they normally stayed outside, particularly as most of the services were inside the relatively cramped confines of crematoria. But during Brian's funeral service, a TV cameraman was inside the crematorium, and had perched himself up in some vantage point to film, which was much to the distress of the relatives, and the anger of some of the mourners.

After the third funeral at the same crematorium, an attendant was handing out cards of the type in which you fill out your name and address for the funerals section of the local newspaper. She handed me 15, saying, 'You'll be needing these.'

For the funeral of Head Waiter, Mick Skippen, the ex-policeman who was awarded a posthumous George Medal for his rescue efforts, suddenly the attitude of the management at Townsend Thoresen started to change. Admittedly the funerals were time-consuming, and all the *Herald* survivors, and many other crew as well, were going to as many as we could. And why should we not have gone?

But the impression we got from the company was that it was all becoming too drawn-out, and was too much of a drain on personnel who were taking constant time off to attend funerals.

The instruction came down to us: 'Only the four people closest to Mick can go.' I said to Charlie Smith, who knew Mick better than I did, 'OK, you be one of the four.'

But the next day, after the funeral, those of us who had not gone felt very badly about it. He was our shipmate, we *should* have gone. And why on earth would any right-thinking company want to stop us? We vowed that we would go to the funerals we wished to attend whether the company liked it or not.

The next funeral was of Steward Alan Medhurst at 2 p.m. on 22 April. Alan had been a very popular man and we all wanted to go. A union representative discussed it with the Master of the ship on which I was now serving. Luckily the Master happened to be a man called Humphrey Craig. I say fortunately because the union representative said to him, 'This ship won't sail. The crew will be at the funerals.' And Craig replied, 'If it doesn't sail it doesn't sail. And if there's anything I can do to help, just ask.'

He agreed to speak to the management, which resulted in a circular being issued asking for relief volunteers so that we could attend the funerals. Such was the feeling, that to my everlasting pride, scores more people than were necessary volunteered. The ship sailed as scheduled, and we went to Alan's funeral at St Paul's Catholic Church, Dover.

I only went to one funeral on a Sunday, that of

Steward Danny Burthe. It was held in a tiny chapel with room for just 30 people. Because of a watch change, Danny had been aboard the *Herald* when in other circumstances he would not have been.

On 23 April there were seven funerals, of which I went to five. I was a pall-bearer at the funeral of my friend David Disbury, one of the three Assistant Pursers aboard the *Herald* that night.

The coffin we bore on our shoulders was bedecked with flowers, some shaped into Teddy bears. It was a strange feeling knowing that above my shoulder, next to my cheek just through the wood of the coffin, lay my friend. We had worked together side by side, and come up through the ranks together. I remembered a stormy clear-the-air crew meeting to discuss grievances, and how under pressure David and I felt. And he had said forcefully, 'I'm not going to be the next Assistant Purser to die from pressures of work.' He was referring to a colleague of ours who had died young. David and I had attended that man's funeral; now it was like seeing a piece of film run twice. Only this time it was David in the coffin.

I thought of him at the meal we had been at in January. He was a happy man, determined not to let his job get him down, determined not to die because of the pressures on him. And despite it all . . .

As we lowered the coffin carefully from our shoulders, I felt the tears streaming down my cheeks. I did not sob or cry out. There would be no awkward scene to distress the relatives. Just silent, unstoppable tears.

Out of the church, into the cars, and on to the crematorium, and as the curtain closed around the coffin, there was that awful finality. I knew then that I would never see David on earth again. It *was* real, it actually *was* happening.

The strain was beginning to take its toll on me now. I was working nights, finishing duty, and then instead of sleeping, I was going to funerals.

On Tuesday, 28 April, I was to go to two funerals, those of John Warwick and Terry Frame, both of whom had been at that January dinner. I was pall-bearer at John's funeral, and afterwards I spoke to his widow. She looked so terribly vulnerable and fragile, but very pretty and her clothes were not too severe. I felt John would have been proud of her that day and I told her so, 'If John is looking down now, he's saying how lovely you look.'

At that funeral, as at some others, I sensed some conflict between widows and parents of the dead. A man might only have been married for a year but automatically it was his wife who was considered the most bereaved. I would not in the least minimise the extent of the grief of the widows. But parents had brought up their sons or daughters from birth, seen them grow from children to adults, and yet in the aftermath of their son or daughter's death, the needs of the parents hardly seemed to be considered.

I think this is something that should be taken account of very seriously, not only after the death of an individual, but certainly following any major tragedy.

Mothers and fathers of the dead, even if those who died had previously been married for years, do deserve great consideration and understanding, because they too grieve terribly.

The next funeral at which I was due to be a pall-bearer was that of Ian Lawson. I could not face carrying his coffin, and I backed out of that task. It was a hot day, I was worn out with tiredness from working nights, and my nerves were frazzled from exhaustion and the constant emotional strain of the funerals.

I felt now that I lived with the daily smell of death. There were the others: Lee Birtles, Catering Storekeeper; Lynda Burt, Stewardess; Bob Crone, Chief Engineer; Graham Evans, Electrical Officer; Steve Ewell, Steward; Barry Head, Steward; John Hobbs, Seaman; Robert Mantle, Radio Officer (whose number 13 I had dialled in vain); Edgerton Quested, Steward; Stephen Sprules, Junior Catering Rating; John Rogers, Motorman; and Stan Darby, Chief Petty Officer Motorman.

The body of Marie Richards, a Stewardess who came from Mauritius, was flown back to her island birthplace in the Southern Indian Ocean. But I attended a personal memorial service for her in Canterbury.

The last funeral I attended was for Graham Evans. Graham had been a part-time fireman, and a wake was held for him in the Fire Station where he had worked.

Because most of the crew lived in the same area a lot of the ceremonies were held at Barham Crematorium. When I drive past it today I still shudder. I felt at the end of those long list of funerals, as I fervently feel now, that I never want to see another coffin or wreath.

I do not believe I could face again as sustained and as concentrated an outpouring of sorrow. It was a bad time; a time of grievance and of widows. I never wish to see the like again.

# 11

## *Back to Sea*

The first communication we had from the company after the disaster told us we could consider ourselves on leave for at least two weeks. No one had broached the subject, either verbally or in writing about my return to the sea, or on what ship. That is, until 25 March. Two letters arrived, one by first post, another by the second post.

The first told me to attend a meeting to discuss joining the *Vortigern*. The second letter, which was clearly meant to have arrived first, explained that the C Watch survivors, with the exception of Petty Officers and Chief Petty Officers, would be transferred to the new ship, *Pride of Dover*, when she went into service on 6 June. Until that time arrangements had been made to charter the *Vortigern* from British Ferries, and I was being put on that vessel on C Watch. Regrettably, the letter went on, because of the smaller size of the *Vortigern*, some *Herald* C Watch people would have to be transferred to other ships. I was to join *Vortigern* on 2 April, to help with cleaning and provisioning, ready for the first sailing on the 8th.

I noticed that on the letters I received the Townsend Thoresen logo was very big in the top left-hand corner, while the P & O logo was discreetly tucked away at the bottom right-hand side. It seemed to me that whenever anything to do with the *Herald* was under discussion the Townsend Thoresen logo was big, and P & O's was small. I am convinced, and I was not the only one, that P & O wanted no association whatsoever with the disaster.

A word of explanation is necessary here, because many people are confused about just who owned the *Herald*. Was it Townsend Thoresen, or was it P & O? And why are we now suing P & O, and not Townsend Thoresen? How do the venerable old company of P & O, with a tradition of 150-odd years, suddenly come into the equation?

Basically what happened was this. In July 1928, Captain Stuart Townsend started the first proper car ferry service between Dover and Calais. In May 1964 Otto Thoresen started a car ferry service between Southampton and Cherbourg. In 1968 the Townsend parent company bought Thoresen, and created Townsend Thoresen European Ferries. The company went from strength to strength. The Atlantic Steam Navigation was added in 1971, and with interests in British ports, property and oil, the future looked rosy.

Oil prices dropped, the company's performance

suffered, and in December 1985, P & O chairman Sir Jeffrey Sterling acquired a 20.8 percent holding in European Ferries. A takeover seemed inevitable, and the inevitable eventually happened on 5 December 1986. Trading of shares in both P & O and European Ferries was suspended on the Stock Exchange on 4 December. The next day shareholders were offered four new P & O shares for 17 of European Ferries.

European Ferries were worth a reported £280 million, and the previous year had turned in a £17 million profit, but strikes had cost them £10 million of that. The bid was worth a reported £448 million, and it was allowed by the Monopolies Commission. Townsend Thoresen European Ferries had new owners.

But to all intents and purposes things went on as normal. Townsend Thoresen was a name the public knew, it had an enterprising record and a distinctive livery of bright orange on its ships. Townsend Thoresen was still used on the side of the ships, and its masthead was distinctive on all correspondence.

The tragedy at Zeebrugge changed all that. Suddenly P & O had a problem on its hands. The mere name 'Townsend Thoresen' was inextricably linked with the capsize at Zeebrugge. The subsequent inquiry with its revelations and its condemnation – 'From top to bottom, the body corporate was affected by the disease of sloppiness ... the failure on the part of the shore management to give proper and clear directions was a contributory cause of the disaster' – became the last straw for P & O.

On 16 July, P & O acted. They scrapped the Townsend Thoresen trading name. It was renamed P & O European Ferries. Ships were to be repainted in P & O Ferries pale blue.

The famous TT logo, known to hundreds of thousands of cross channel passengers, was to disappear as soon as was possible.

P & O blamed the 'negative effect' of the Townsend Thoresen name for the change. It was hard to argue with that from their point of view, but we felt a little differently. It was clear the change had been no spur-of-the-moment decision. In the July issue of *Sea Breezes* ('The Magazine of Ships and the Sea'), writer John F. Hendy described a crossing he had made to Zeebrugge in May. He wrote:

> '... the last of the Townsend Thoresen fleet was in the process of having her funnels painted in the P & O Ferries livery. The speed with which this was done was remarkable, and a job which would normally have waited until the end of the season was completed in a fortnight.
>
> 'P & O clearly wish to distance themselves from Townsend Thoresen, and their advertisements state, "For over 150 years ... we have gained a tradition of operational standards second to none." The inference is clear enough – with P & O in charge such a disaster is unlikely to occur again.
>
> 'The implication, along with the repainting of the funnels, has upset many Townsend Thoresen

employees, who have much to be proud of in a company which in the last two decades, has been the most successful of all British ferry operators.'

Hendy had it dead right. Zeebrugge was to be forgotten, and the crew who had been there, tolerated only as long as they did not make a fuss, and as long as they ceased to say or do anything that would remind people of the *Herald*.

The day before I received my two letters from the company I should have been at a Marine Escapes System course at Dover, on a course concerned with how to operate escape shutes. I had been invited two weeks earlier, but there was no follow up reminder, and as far as I know the course was never held. Things were in a turmoil, and day to day things were being overlooked.

In the meantime I had to have some physiotherapy on my shoulder. I had wrenched it badly during the rescue work at Zeebrugge, and now it was giving me quite a lot of pain.

My date for joining the *Vortigern* had been put back until 8 p.m. on Saturday 4 April. But I did not intend to wait for my first day on active duty to see if I could face the sea again.

A small group of us got together, picked a day, and decided to make a crossing. The ship we chose was the *Spirit of Free Enterprise*, an almost identical ship to the *Herald*. The interior layout and design, in particular, is exactly the same as the *Herald*. We sailed at noon on 30 March for Calais.

It is hard to describe how I felt. Eerie is the best word for the moment I stepped on board. It was like going back in time. The effect of what we had all been through showed in the most practical way. The first thing we did was to check the nearest exits.

Suddenly, in mid Channel, the ship slowed and we heard the chop-chop of a helicopter's rotor blades. It was a chilling sound to us. The last time we had heard it was over the stricken *Herald* as rescue helicopters hovered, winching off survivors.

Everyone rushed out on deck. What was it? What was the emergency? My heart pounded, I could feel the rush of blood around my body, surely we could not be hit by *another* accident?

A crewman was lowered on a winch, and my heart was in my mouth as I saw him stroll through the lounge, helmet in hand. But it was simply an exercise, he smiled and waved to the passengers. The helicopter was an RAF one from Manston, Kent, and it was a rehearsal for emergency situations.

I was shocked and angry. The company knew we were on board that day, a group of survivors putting their guts on the line and going out to sea for the first time since an appalling maritime tragedy. Could they not have picked another ship and another day for the helicopter exercise? Or at the very least could they not have warned us it was going to happen?

If any announcement was made over the Tannoy to

the effect that the whole thing was an exercise, we certainly never heard it. The general impressions of the rest of the passengers seemed to bear out the fact that, until they saw the winchman smiling and waving, they thought they were witnessing a real emergency. It was another failure of the company's compassion and imagination.

I went to the Purser's Office on C Deck, and he asked me how I had escaped at Zeebrugge, and I told him. Eventually a group of us *Herald* crewmen sat down together. We were all very jittery, and one or two were totally wound up. We had one lad under 18 with us, Danny Wyman, a Junior Catering Rating, who made the decision not to return to life at sea after that day. Two of the older people in the party also made the same decision.

Later during the trip I went back to the Information Office and gazed at the escape route I had followed when the *Herald* went over. In daylight, with the ship at its correct angle, it looked so innocent and so easy. The passageway to the ladies' loo, the door through which I might have fallen – everything was normal now. I reached the passageway that crosses the ship. On the *Herald* it had turned from that into a deadly shaft across which I had to jump for my life. Now it was an innocent passageway again.

I was so bound up with nerves that I could not eat, although I managed to drink a couple of halves of lager. Two Pursers had come along to accompany us, just in case the ordeal proved too much for any of us. One was a man called Bob Jarvis. I confess that up to that moment I had always found Bob an unsympathetic sort of bloke, but on that day he was kind and understanding. In fact, his performance in dealing with us was brilliant. The weather was fine, the sea normal, but I became very conscious of the Tannoy announcements, especially after the unexpected arrival of the rescue helicopter.

I wandered over to the restaurant area and walked about it fascinated. I marvelled at how anyone at all managed to get out of it after the capsize. And I still thought of those who had died on the *Herald*.

When the ship reached Calais we stayed on board, and returned on the homeward leg to Dover. Despite everything I was glad I had made the trip.

I had been very nervous, checking exits, listening for Tannoy announcements, but I had managed to cope, even with the helicopter incident. It made me aware that I could set foot on board a ship, even one as ghostily familiar as this, without cracking up. So, I reasoned, I could go back to my job, buckle down, screw up my courage and carry on.

But this was to be an illusion – or so it proved to be in the long run. For these were early days, and things were not getting better with me. They were getting worse.

# 12

## *My God, It's Going to Split*

I think some people felt we survivors were obsessed with what happened at Zeebrugge, and that we did not even try to forget it at the time. But even if we had wished to, or had been capable of it, we were not allowed to. Even without the funerals and the memorial services, there were the little irritants that began to creep in.

Speculation was rife, and everyone seemed to have a theory about what had happened. Rumours abounded.

In early April the *Daily Mirror* carried a story saying that John Butler, the Car Deck Steward, had given a clear two-minute warning that water was flowing over the car deck, but that the warning had not reached the Master of the vessel. It was common knowledge that I was the individual who had taken John's telephone call. The clear implication was that I had failed to pass on the warning.

That was untrue, as the inquiry would later make very clear. I had no sooner taken John's call and put out a Tannoy for the ship's carpenter, than the *Herald* rolled over.

Why were people jumping to wrong and potentially damaging conclusions before they knew the facts?

A photographer claiming to be from the *Daily Mirror* knocked on my door and asked if he could take my picture. When I told him he could not, he said in an aggrieved tone, 'But I've driven all the way from London.'

Finally I joined the *Vortigern* on 9 April. She was in need of a good spring clean, and she got it. The next day we sailed for Boulogne, with me at my post in the Information Office.

It seemed strange to be back in harness and occupied. Those of us *Herald* C Watch survivors on board went around reassuring one another. But once, when the weather became quite rough, I noticed that all of us were as near to the exits as we could possibly get. I suppose this was understandable.

Zeebrugge just would not leave us alone though. A girl started writing to me. She lived in Leytonstone in East London and was convinced that I had once been her boyfriend. I had no idea who she was, and I had never met her in my life. In fact at the time she suggested we had been going out together, in 1966, I was only 14 years old! But she persisted. She had seen me, or read about me, during the press and TV coverage of the disaster, and she would not leave me alone.

She sent me notes pleading with me to meet her. I did not reply, but my silence did not seem to deter her. At first I did not tell Anne because I did not want to upset her, but later I took her into my confidence. One day the letter writer turned up at the P & O personnel office in Dover. Failing to get any response from me with letters, she had decided to try the personal touch. I was told that she was waiting to see me, but I refused point blank to have anything to do with her. Perhaps she was just genuinely mistaken, but more possibly she was a disturbed woman. I did not wish to discover which.

I had enough on my mind without this. I told the personnel office, 'You deal with it, it's nothing to do with me.'

Next I received a telephone call from a man who said he worked on a building site, and was a friend of the letter-writer. He was very annoyed and demanded to know why I had not been in contact with her. I told him firmly, 'I don't know her.' He said, 'But she's going crazy over this.' I was adamant that I would not have any involvement with her whatsoever. I felt that the first time I made any acknowledgement of her existence – even if only to deny that I ever knew her – she would only be more encouraged.

My firmness on the telephone seemed to work, for to my tremendous relief the letters stopped, and there was not another call from her friend on the building site.

It had been an extra annoyance, and it had played on my nerves. At home I was irritable, uncommunicative, and quick to lose my temper. I do not know how Anne put up with me.

I found it very hard to actually finish a meal, and as

a result I was still unable to put my lost weight back on. It had dropped by a stone, and I have yet to regain it. I was depressed and nervy. And there was still the national memorial service to come.

The national memorial service was to be held on 15 April at Canterbury Cathedral, and would be broadcast live on BBC TV. Anne and I received invitations, and Terry Ayling and myself had agreed to lay a cross of flowers at the altar.

Terry and I had rehearsed our walk the day prior to the ceremony at the request of the Cathedral authorities, walking slowly side by side down the great aisle and up to the altar.

But on the day itself we came inches from a débâcle that would have been seen by millions watching the live broadcast, and marred the solemnity of the occasion. A fracture developed in the foam base of the cross that supported the flowers. As we walked I could feel the cross beginning to give. I thought 'My God, it's going to split'.

Terry and I began to walk, as slowly as possible, past the dignitaries, past Neil Kinnock and Margaret Thatcher, and on towards Princess Anne and the Duke of Edinburgh. All I could think of was 'What if it splits?' In my imagination I could see it dividing in two, and the top half of the floral cross bending slowly over.

But thank God it held. We laid it on the altar steps and Terry and I stood stock still to attention. We had been told to wait for a long and solemn interval, then turn and retrace our steps. Terry had agreed to wait for me to turn, then turn with me. The walk had calmed my nerves and pounding heart a little. But Terry, in his nervousness, turned rather too soon, so naturally I had to follow, and we both went back to our seats.

I could not help noticing as we walked back under the eyes of the cameras, the amount of VIPs, such as Mayors and Mayoresses from towns all over Britain, who were in the congregation.

Survivors and their families had been denied the best vantage points, and been dotted around the Cathedral to make way for these civic dignitaries. It always seems the way that those with the least involvement or reason for being at such an occasion, are treated as though they have the most importance.

I imagine that those dignitaries represented towns in which some of the victims had lived. Nonetheless, I did not think they should have had priority over survivors and the bereaved.

It was clear that this service was not personal to those from the *Herald* or those who had lost friends or families. Even the invitation Anne and I received enclosed a list of hotels in Canterbury, and directions 'for those unfamiliar with the city'. Most of the *Herald* crew families lived less than 20 miles away, and Canterbury was a familiar place for them. The arrangements were impersonal, and catered more for the needs of those outside the area.

The service itself was quite moving. I am not a religious man, but the effect of the hymns and the sermon was a calming one. Because of the shape of the Cathedral, not everyone could actually see all the service, but monitor sets had been put up at various points by the BBC.

The service started with 'Eternal Father, strong to save, whose arm hath bound the restless wave.' It was after this moving hymn that Terry and I laid the wreath before the Nave altar, and candles were lit.

Later the Archbishop of Canterbury, Robert Runcie, gave his sermon. He highlighted some of the heroic acts at Zeebrugge, and then spoke of the families and friends of those who had died: 'For them the tragedies remain. And with it the numbness of loss and grief. The tragedy was so sudden, the loss so unexpected. To those who carry this burden of pain we offer our deepest sympathy. And no sympathy will, I know, be so heartfelt as the sympathy of those who shared the horrors of that night but came through unhurt, and with their families and friends unharmed.'

P & O released us from work to attend the rehearsals for the ceremony that Wednesday, and I am grateful to them for that. It was an honour and privilege to lay the wreath.

I managed to speak to the Archbishop, Dr Runcie, shortly before the service, but afterwards it was a different story. Entrance to the reception held following the memorial service was by invitation only. And as far as we ordinary crew members were concerned we could forget it. Only Masters and Senior Officers with P & O were asked. Instead outsiders with nothing to do with the *Herald*, or probably the sea, and with no other position than their qualification and status, were invited.

Those of us who had actually *been* there that night, were not. Yes, we felt bitter. And if you think I harp on that, imagine how you would feel in similar circumstances. Suddenly, however solemn the service was, it became a social occasion, with positions and status to be considered. And those with a direct personal involvement were relegated and shut out. Wouldn't you have been bitter?

We all headed back to Dover where the National Union of Seamen had laid on a small 'do' for us at the Moat House Hotel in Townhall Street. The Union's General Secretary, Sam McCluskie, was waiting to greet us. We ate and supped with those willing to welcome us. People who really understood what we were going through.

# 13

## *Oh, Canada*

Anne and I celebrated our second wedding anniversary quietly at home on 11 May. Neither of us felt particularly like going out, and I was still very depressed and querulous. But four days later, Anne, Simon and myself left Gatwick airport on a DC 10 for Toronto for our long-awaited holiday. We had really looked forward to it, but what with Zeebrugge and the following traumatic weeks, its importance became magnified for me. I could hardly wait to get away.

Every day, or so it seemed, there was something in a newspaper or a radio or TV broadcast, that mentioned the tragedy. If I went into town I would see people I knew and try to avoid them. So many people were stopping me, saying, 'What was it like, Steve?' And I could not take this. I used to dodge into shops to hide, anything not to have to talk about the *Herald*.

My brother Clifford had moved to Canada, married a lovely Canadian girl, Debbie, and bought a house in

Toronto. They were both at the airport to see us and we had a marvellous reunion.

The early summer weather was glorious. It was warm and the sky was a clear blue. After a few days in Toronto we all made the three-hour car trip to Hastings, Ontario, where Debbie's parents live.

We had use of a canoe with an outboard motor, and while Debbie kindly looked after Simon for us, Cliff, Anne and I went out on the lakes and rivers. It was a world away from Folkestone and Dover. A world away from the grey Channel, from ferries and funeral services. It was totally peaceful. There were no blaring radios or cars, just tranquillity, peace and solitude. And after cluttered England there seemed to be so much space. Vast stretches of water, like glass it was so still. Forests that seemed to go on for eternity.

We saw fish, and porcupine, and beaver. The beavers were amazing, slapping their tails on the water with a resounding crack to warn of our approach.

We stayed at a beautiful wooden lodge deep in the forests and lakes of the region, its balcony jutting out over a lake. We sat in the lounge with an unrivalled view across the mirror-like surface of the water, and watched humming-birds nibbling and pecking at food we had put out for them. No fences or parked cars, no hedges or limits, just seemingly boundless space.

We went to lots of picnics, and revelled in the free-and-easy Canadian lifestyle, so different from our own rather reserved and insular manner. I slept soundly for the first time since the capsize. So intoxicated were we both with Canada, that Anne and I talked about moving there and starting afresh. In the end we decided against it. Both of us are close to our families in Britain, and neither felt we could uproot ourselves and cut ourselves off. I felt this especially, having learnt through tragedy just how dear to me they were.

We went on a trip to Niagara Falls, a couple of hours from Toronto, and watched all the mighty water thundering over. I had a great respect for water's awesome weight and power, and could only marvel at this natural wonder of the world.

We had a memorable weekend planned for our final days in North America. We took the train to New York! It was an 11-hour trip from Toronto – we will never complain about British Rail again – and we seemed to trundle along at 20 miles an hour. At Schenectady in New York State, we broke our journey to stay with friends. Immediately it was out with the barbecue and on with the steaks. The gin and tonics were mammoth and the evening was a roaring success.

We caught the train by the skin of our teeth, and next it was on to Manhattan. We stayed at the Penta Hotel, opposite the Penn Central station, and did all the usual touristy things. Both of us were excited by the Big Apple, as Americans call New York. It had a tremendous vitality and buzz that we both liked. We went to the World Trade Centre, trendy and bohemian Greenwich Village, and even made the four-and-something hour trip around the island of Manhattan by Circle Line boat. It was a great boat trip, marred only by the fact that the man giving the commentary starts at the beginning and never stops until the boat does. He gives you every detail, including how many rivets are in every bridge under which you sail!

At Pier 88 on the Hudson River there was an aircraft carrier and a Royal Viking Line cruise ship tied up. I knew my maritime history. In its time, Pier 88 had seen some of the most famous Transatlantic liners in the world. Liners like the *Queen Mary*, now a floating resort and exhibition at Long Beach in California, like the *Normandie* and the *Isle de France*. Liners had battled each other in prestige runs to see who could make the crossing fastest, and passengers lived in a kind of luxury probably impossible to reproduce now.

And now on Pier 88 there was just an aircraft carrier and a 'Love-Boat' ready to take sun-starved New Yorkers down to Miami and the Bahamas. The sea and its ships are constantly changing.

We trundled slowly back from New York, and I spent the long hours chatting to a Chinese man who had come from Communist China to study pollution control.

In Toronto we said our goodbyes and boarded the flight back. It was time to return to normality. But Canada had been good for me. The peace and quiet, the fresh air, the new vistas, all served to both soothe and stimulate me in the right ways. I felt considerably better than I had since the tragedy, and the timing of the trip seemed like a Godsend. A psychiatrist was to tell me later that our Canada trip almost certainly saved me from an immediate and complete breakdown.

But the benefit I got from that holiday only seemed to provide a temporary respite. Before I went there my consumption of alcohol had increased, though it was mainly beer and only rarely spirits. In Canada, with the exception of the odd pre-dinner gin and tonic, or a glass of wine with meals, I hardly drank. I was not taking any drugs at all, and even though my doctor offered me something (probably Valium) to help me sleep. I had declined. I did not want to get into the habit of taking tranquillisers.

I certainly never contemplated suicide, not even at my lowest ebb. It would have been ludicrous, if not obscene, to have gone through all that happened on the *Herald*, and then to have taken my own life.

Sometimes it is harder to survive and live, than to give up and die. It would have been an insult to those who *had* died, and to those who had bravely clawed their way to survival, to give up my life voluntarily and without a fight.

If I learned anything from Zeebrugge it was just how valuable life is, how precious and dear a commodity: it should be treasured. There is poverty and war, disease and catastrophe all over the world, so those of us who have life must cherish and value it properly.

But my grief and the strain were very real, not only to me, but to those who knew me. Masters of the ships on which I sailed seemed reluctant to discuss Zeebrugge.

There was this strong and recurring feeling within me that as the weeks dragged on people like me were becoming an increasing embarrassment. So more and more we turned inwards, towards the band of other survivors.

Billy Fothergill, a Purser on the *Herald*, though not on C Watch, used to sit with me in his cabin on the *Pride of Free Enterprise*, and discuss the tragedy with me. It occupied my every waking thought again. There was the major inquiry to come, and a separate police inquiry. There seemed no end to it all.

Gail Cook organised a social evening for the survivors, at the Railway Club in Dover. We had little badges made up, a gold-rimmed circle with the points of the compass, and the words, '*Herald of Free Enterprise*, C Watch – Always Remembered'.

Mark Stanley was there. Mark was the man who admitted being asleep, and failing to close the bow doors. It was not the first time I had seen him since Zeebrugge. A few of us would meet up in a Dover pub called 'The Mogul' for a drink and a chat. Sometimes Mark would be in there, as would David Lewry, the Master on duty that night of 6 March.

As far as I know not one single member of the crew ever railed against Mark for what he had done – or rather, had failed to do. We knew he was going through a living hell. He had an unbelievable burden to carry, and we knew he would be weighed down with it for the rest of his life.

Relatives of the dead could also be forgiving. Glen's parents wrote to Mark telling him they did not hold anything against him for what had happened. A grateful and emotional Mark wrote back thanking them.

People have asked me since, whether as an individual who came close to death, and who lost close friends on the *Herald*, I am bitter or angry towards Mark in particular.

The answer is No. He was a victim of circumstance, a small link in a chain, a cog in a machine, a part of a system. I blame that system and the people who administered it. Why were *repeated* requests for some kind of bow door warning device ignored? Why was there not a one to ten countdown, a checklist just like they have on aeroplanes pre-flight? No plane would roll down the runway with its flaps in the wrong position, with one engine not switched on. So how could it be conceivable for a ship to move away into *its* hostile and potentially deadly environment, without a similar check, and a confirmation from a second party that things were in order?

Mark has to live with his part in what happened. I hope those people in Townsend Thoresen management who bear responsibility for ignoring those memos, can live with what *they* did. For it was they who set the scene for an accident that was only waiting for a moment of human error, to happen.

If I have bitterness and anger – and I have both – it is for those presumably unnamed and unvillified individuals, and not for Mark Stanley.

# 14

# *And We Died Like Rabbits, Too*

A careless word or thoughtless jibe can really sting and hurt. One that moved me to tears of anger happened aboard the *Vortigern*. Charles Smith and I from C Watch were the two Assistant Pursers, and we were joined by Barry Wick. Barry had been an Assistant Purser on the *Herald*, but not our watch. He had done tireless work at Zeebrugge, and been to the mortuary and witnessed some distressing sights when the *Herald* was finally raised and the bodies recovered. So upset was Barry that he was given some time off to recover. As he stood with Charles and I on the *Vortigern*, a Catering Superintendent called Chris Rowden came up and said, 'Cor, you breed like rabbits don't you?'

Perhaps Chris had not meant anything by it, and perhaps he just meant Assistant Pursers in general. But to me at that time it said everything about how I felt *Herald* people were regarded. We were a problem, something that had to be shifted from ship to ship. Would it, I wondered bitterly, have been tidier if we had all gone down with the ship? It welled up inside me and I turned on the man, tears of anger in my eyes, fury in my voice. I said, 'Yes – and we died like rabbits too.' Chris made himself scarce very quickly.

I was due to appear at the official inquiry on 29 April, its third day. I went up to London by train with Terry Ayling and Mark Stanley. Each of us bought a First Class ticket so we would not be in a crowded carriage, and so we could chat freely without being the object of any morbid interest.

Considering the emotional state he must have been in, Mark was remarkably calm. He was being constantly pestered, his telephone never stopped ringing, and he was frequently approached by the press. It was a wonder he had not had a nervous breakdown, given the burden he was carrying. For it was now public knowledge that it was Mark who had failed to close the bow doors. He never tried to shirk responsibility for what had happened. I have written how, on the night of the tragedy, he stood on the capsized hull, saying over and over, 'I left the doors open.'

When he was interviewed by investigators Mark gave a full and frank account of his negligence. Somehow the newspapers had discovered that, and then the world and his wife knew, and attention was then focused on Mark.

The three of us took a taxi from Charing Cross railway station in London, to Church House, Westminster, where the inquiry was being held. We went in by a side door to avoid the horde of photographers taking pictures of people at the main entrance.

Carpenter Mick Tracey gave his evidence, and then it was my turn. (I had seen John Butler there. Although his wife was having a baby any day then, he had been ordered to attend.)

I could feel the familiar symptoms of nervousness: sweating palms, wildly beating heart, that rush of adrenalin as I faced the inquiry and Mr Justice Sheen.

He and his panel were in front; around me there was what felt like a crescent of lawyers, some representing the passengers, others P & O, some the National Union of Seamen.

The atmosphere was very official, and extremely correct. I was asked to give a brief account of the day, the run-up to the capsize, and then the actual event itself.

My evidence lasted between 30 and 40 minutes, and I tried not to be too graphic for I did not wish to add to the suffering of any bereaved who might be present. I made a point of telling the inquiry that the emergency lighting had either been non-existent, or at best totally inadequate. I told how the buoyancy of the scattered lifejackets was a hindrance to people trying to get out of the water and on to escape ladders or ropes.

I suggested a safety harness similar to those used by rescue helicopters. If those were kept as rescue equipment on ships in the event of similar capsizes, people who had been in the water could be hauled up without them slipping out of ropes tied around them.

Mr Justice Sheen asked me how the crew had acted on that night. My reply was, 'Herculean would be an understatement.' I have rarely meant anything more in my life.

A lawyer from P & O seemed to be obsessed with the ship's bag, asking me where I had got the tonnage figure I telephoned to the bridge. I had already told the inquiry about that. So I replied, 'I thought I had made myself perfectly clear.'

I was not the only crew member to give evidence at the inquiry who felt that the P & O lawyers appeared to be treating us with downright hostility, and we resented this attitude.

I found the whole thing harrowing. At one point I could feel my voice breaking with emotion. I paused and drank some water, felt better, and was able to continue.

I was very aware that every word that each witness uttered was for the record, and there would be no second chance to tell *exactly* what had happened.

I was relieved when it was all over.

I noticed that although lawyers representing the passengers thanked us for our efforts in helping the passengers, at no time when I was present did the P & O lawyers acknowledge our role.

At the lunch adjournment I was approached by a female reporter from ITN who wanted an interview, but I refused as I felt I had answered enough questions that day.

The official findings, when finally published in July,

were scathing about the senior management of Townsend Thoresen. The *Herald*, it seemed, had sailed with both its bow *and* stern doors open.

The *Daily Telegraph* of 25 July carried a large report of the proceedings in which Mr Justice Sheen said the 29-day inquiry had revealed Townsend Thoresen as a company 'infected with the disease of sloppiness' from top to bottom. He added that although errors and omissions by some of the crew members and officers on board the *Herald* were clear faults leading to the disaster, there was a more deep-rooted problem.

'The board of directors,' Mr Justice Sheen stated, 'did not have any proper comprehension of what their duties were. There appears to have been a lack of thought about the way in which the *Herald* ought to have been reorganised for the Dover–Zeebrugge run.' He added that all concerned in management, from the members of the board of directors down to the junior superintendents were guilty of fault, in that all must be regarded as sharing responsibility for the failure of management.

He also attacked management for showing, 'staggering complacency'. He said that suggestions put forward by the company's Masters, fell on deaf ears. And four in particular:

- Complaints that ships were carrying passengers in excess of the permitted number.
- The request to have lights fitted on the bridge to

indicate whether the bow and stern doors were open or closed.

- Draught (depth) marks could not be read, and ships were not provided with instruments for reading draughts. At times ships were required to arrive and sail from Zeebrugge trimmed by the head without any relevant stability information.
- The request to have a high capacity ballast pump to deal with the trimming ballast.

Mr Justice Sheen specifically attributed blame to the Master, Captain David Lewry, Assistant Bosun Mark Stanley, and First Officer Leslie Sabel.

The inquiry suggested also that the Department of Transport might wish to consider whether it should be an offence for a ship to leave with its doors open.

As a matter of urgency, the report went on, all roll-on, roll-off ferries should be fitted with a self-contained water-tight lighting system. Reliable and uncomplicated escape windows should be fitted, designed to open from inside or out. Exits and lifejacket stores should be prominently labelled.

The company was ordered to pay a staggering £400,000 towards the inquiry costs. This was on top of the estimated £750,000 the company spent on legal representation for the 29-day hearing.

Mr Justice Sheen said that the company had to bear a heavy responsibility for the disaster, and the inquiry had no other way to mark its feelings about Townsend

Thoresen's conduct, other than by ordering it to pay a substantial part of the costs.

Of the £400,000 awarded, the Department of Transport was to receive £350,000, with the other £50,000 to go to the National Union of Seamen, which had represented crew members who survived, and the families of victims.

The inquiry demanded immediate action including indicator lights to ensure that the doors were closed (in fact this had been done immediately after the tragedy), and a 'fail-safe' system. The fact that the doors had been closed should always be entered in the ship's log.

The *Daily Telegraph* reported also that the company chairman, Peter Ford, said Mr Justice Sheen was right to make 'tough and pungent comments about management of the company and the individuals involved'. He continued:

> 'We have reconstituted the management. We have instituted completely new operational safety procedures in the fleet, including new ship-to-shore reporting and management systems.
>
> 'We are taking part in a technical enquiry into roll-off, roll-on ships in conjunction with the Department of Transport, Lloyd's Register, and the General Council of British Shipping.'

The stable door was now firmly bolted.

The two British seafaring unions reacted angrily to

the report, and what it considered to be its failings. The National Union of Seamen said it was 'disappointed' that no legal action was to be taken against Townsend Thoresen, which was responsible for the safe operation of the *Herald of Free Enterprise*. The NUS said also it was unhappy that no reference had been made in the report to the Department of Transport's ineffectiveness as an enforcement agency. Finally, it considered that it was unfair to single out individuals for reprimand or punishment in the context of such a disaster.

Eric Nevin the general secretary of NUMAST, the officers' union, said bitterly, 'Why should two officers be selected for punishment when there is a complex chain of responsibility for the disaster? The scapegoat system is not what I recognise as British justice.'

Captain Lewry had had his Master's certificate suspended for a year, and First Officer Leslie Sabel had his certificate suspended for two years.

Mr Nevin added that regarding ship design, equipment and procedures, many people bore responsibility; naval architects, the Department of Transport, insurers and the rest of the shipping community.

'Only in terms of attention to duty in a rushed situation caused by the failure of those august bodies, did two officers and one rating have involvement in the complex chain. Why then should those two individual officers be singled out as scapegoats? Apparently to purge the guilt of a whole community which has failed,' he commented.

In the House of Commons, Transport Secretary Paul

Channon said new legislation would be drawn up to make it a criminal offence for a ferry to sail with her deck doors open. He also pledged £1 million towards an enhanced research programme into the stability of roll-on, roll-off ferries, and the implications of additional bulk-heads.

Two of the harshly criticised individuals responded after the inquiry findings. Captain Lewry, his wife Patricia at his side, said, 'My deepest sympathy goes to all those people who lost family and friends on the *Herald of Free Enterprise* that night. Obviously a lot of the crew were my friends as well, and some of the crew had sailed together for several years.'

Mr Justice Sheen had said that no doubt Mark Stanley would suffer remorse for some considerable time.

Mark showed just how much when he gave his first-ever interview since the tragedy. He said he had known as soon as the ship started to roll over, that he had left the doors open. 'All these stories came out that she could have hit a breakwater, or a big rock in the Channel. That wasn't a glimmer of hope to me at all, because I knew all the time it was the doors. Everyone was asking each other what had happened, and I knew what had happened, but I wasn't going to tell anyone down there '

(In fact, Mark may not remember it, but he *did* keep saying at the time, 'I left the doors open.')

Mark continued, 'I was hoping everyone would get off. When I got on the tug I saw people coming in injured, and I realised there would be loss of life. At the time I was thinking of ten or a dozen ... not that it would have mattered, because it was still loss of life.

'I shall always carry guilt, whatever the others' responsibilities were, it was my responsibility to shut the doors – as simple as that. It's not up to me to blame anyone else, and I'm not going to.'

Mark continued that there were times when he thought his world had ended, 'You thought, how can I ever live with this? You can, in the end.' Mark said that if he met survivors or relatives he would not know what to say; saying sorry just was not enough.

The inquiry also gave the full and stark technical reasons why the *Herald* sank. As we know now its bow and stern doors were open when it sailed. The speed of the vessel, said the inquiry report, went up to about 18 knots.

> 'Towards the end of the acceleration the combination of dynamic sinkage, or squat, and an increase in bow wave caused water to enter over the spade, and flow after into G deck. The court is satisfied the rate of inflow of water was large and increased progressively as the ship dug the bow spade deeper into the water and decreased the freeboard forward. A large quantity of water entered G deck and caused an initial lurch to port due to free surface instability which was extremely rapid and reached perhaps 30 degrees. The water collected in the port wing of the vehicle deck and the ship became stable again at a large angle of roll. Water in large quantities continued to flood

through the open bow doors aperture. Thereafter the *Herald* capsized to port rather more slowly, and eventually she was at more than 90 degrees. It is not possible to say whether the ship reached more than 90 degrees while still floating, or whether this was only when she reached the sea bed. There is some reason for thinking the ship floated more or less on her beam ends for about a minute before finally resting on the sea bed.'

In layman's terms what had happened was that the *Herald* had gone out of harbour with a gaping hole in her bow caused by the open doors. She was also loaded and tilting forward at the front. As her speed increased, the 'spade' – the bow door ramp – was pushed into the water, scooping up the bow wave and allowing hundreds and thousands of gallons of sea water to pour in.

This water settled on the port side, causing the first roll. Then the ship steadied. But as more water rushed in, the extra weight sent the ship into its final death roll. It probably floated on its side for a minute before finally settling on the sandbank that saved it from turning completely turtle.

Had it not been for the sandbank there would have been none of us left to give evidence to the inquiry. A short while after we attended the inquiry Townsend Thoresen did a re-creation of the fatal trip out of Zeebrugge, ostensibly to see what kind of bow wave would be thrown up in that speed and situation.

I watched it on TV that night, seeing the bow wave curling up. The bow doors of the ship they used, the *Pride of Free Enterprise*, were of course, firmly shut. But it was easy to see just how much water would have poured into any ferry with its doors open. It was a terrifying amount.

Seeing the re-creation was a chilling experience. It was like going back to the night of the tragedy, only seeing it as it might have happened.

As we worked obliviously, the *Herald* had been ploughing up that enormous bow wave, and instead of it being scythed by the bow, it had been engorged by the hungry mouth that was the open bow doors.

It made my blood run cold.

# 15

## *Not Brave – Stupid!*

Shortly after my return from Canada I was instructed to join the ship *Pride of Free Enterprise*. The *Pride* was a sister ship of the *Herald*, and identical in almost every way. Going aboard was like going back in time, a weird and ghostly feeling. It was as though 6 March had never come, the tragedy had not happened, and everything was as it had been. I was haunted by a feeling that suddenly I would see a familiar face, people I knew, people with whom I had worked and been happy.

I would walk up to one of the selling points, and for a split second I would literally forget about Zeebrugge and instead look out for a former colleague; then just as suddenly I would realise that person was now dead. This happened often.

I found my cabin, and it was exactly the same as the one I had used on the *Herald*, but of course it did not have the small personal touches I had added, like the cassette system. No Mozart or Pavarotti or Elizabethan

Serenade, no leather shoulder bag with the spare shirt. All those possessions were now just debris on the raised *Herald*.

On one voyage a Mrs Woodhouse, who had lost a son on the *Herald*, asked to be shown around. The ship's Master, Dave Matthews, knew that I was on duty, but obviously did not remember that I was a Zeebrugge survivor, for he rang down to me and said in a rather brusque manner, 'We've got one of those people from the inquest, I want you to show her around.'

Just another one of those people from the inquest. So that was how relatives of the people who had died on the *Herald* were being referred to.

And no matter that *I* might find it distressing showing her around the ship.

I met the woman, who was accompanied by a female friend, and I took them on a tour of the vessel. You could see the strain on the bereaved woman's face, and she looked as though she had had to take some medication to get her through what was clearly a struggle for her. Her friend said, 'It's been a terrible ordeal.' I replied, 'I know, I was on that ship too.' I just could not help getting involved.

Mrs Woodhouse asked if she could throw some flowers over the port side, and I took them down Number Four stairway, and stepped back to let them have their private moment.

She gently tossed a couple of roses into the water. Then she said, 'I'd like to see the bow doors.' I took her below deck, and she gazed at those mammoth steel doors. Then she looked at me and said sadly but nervously, 'How is it they could leave those doors open?'

I replied, 'I've been looking for the answer to that question myself. And if I knew it, it would solve a lot of things for me.'

She turned away and continued gazing at the doors, as though they might yield an answer. As I walked up the gangway with the two women, Mrs Woodhouse's companion said, 'You must be very brave coming back to work on a vessel like this.'

I answered, 'Not brave – stupid!'

I found it an unnerving experience to suddenly be touched by someone else's deep grief. And clearly this woman and her companion were tormented by the same things I was.

It is the nature of things that one month's tragedy is the next month's subject for humour. Perhaps it is a reflex safety action, that when you have ceased crying, you start laughing.

It was not that way for me, but it seemed that the general public had quickly adapted. And if it was not humour, it was natural curiosity. Both were wounding.

We would get coachloads of kids on board, and the first thing they would say was, 'Hey, this is just like the one that went over with its doors open.' Not once did I hear that remark, but *hundreds* of times.

Men would laugh and shout to me before we sailed, 'Hope you've got those doors shut, mate.' Each person who said it perhaps imagined they were the first. But each trip, backwards and forwards between Dover and Calais, it was the same thing, week in and week out.

And it wore on you like the persistent drip-drip of a leaking tap, until you wanted to scream at them to shut up. Because it was not a joke to me, and would never be; it could never be a subject for a flippant aside.

When I used the Tannoy I was very careful, if I was calling for the ship's carpenter – the last message I had relayed on the *Herald* – to use my softest, least alarmist voice. For there was always someone on board who knew the details of the tragedy inside out, and if I made that announcement quickly or urgently, they would assume we had water pouring into the ship.

On one trip a typical holidaymaker came up to the Information Office and asked me whether the engine room watertight compartment doors were closed. There had been a programme on a local TV station that questioned whether P & O followed the procedure of Belgian ships, which was to seal off the various engine room compartments with the watertight doors closed while at sea. That would greatly reduce the risk of the ship sinking if she was damaged in a collision that left the crew little time to get the doors shut.

I told the passenger that honestly I did not know, but that I would find out. I was conscious of a company memo pointing out to us that from now on our behaviour on board, particularly in terms of safety, would obviously be closely watched by the public. It had urged us to take the greatest care acting in responsibly and giving no cause for alarm. So in the passenger's presence I dialled the bridge.

The ship's Master, Captain Joe Stoker answered, and I told him, 'I've just had a passenger enquire whether watertight doors are closed on the voyage.'

The Master was clearly not amused at being interrupted minutes before our departure. Tersely he told me, 'Tell the passenger they *are* shut, and if anyone else asks in future tell *them* they're shut.'

After I left P & O, former colleagues told me that a memo had been sent around by the management requesting crew not to discuss the Zeebrugge tragedy with passengers, even if the passengers asked a direct question.

The old slipshod ways had not really improved, either. An incident occurred which was terrifying in its implications. What happened was probably not, in itself, dangerous but in view of what had befallen the *Herald* it was almost unthinkable. A ferry moved with its doors open!

The *Daily Mirror* in a page one story revealed in early May, that the P & O ferry *Free Enterprise 7* had made a short trip – while still in harbour – with its bow doors open. The story was then raised in the European Parliament, and angry Labour Euro MPs demanded a full-scale European Economic Community investigation. The ship's Master, Captain John Marks gave evidence to an internal inquiry at Dover.

In the House of Commons, Transport Secretary Paul Channon told questioning MPs that he was carrying out his own investigation into the 'important allegation.' But, in what I believe was an astonishingly complacent remark, he said MPs' fears were 'overstating it.' And he confirmed that the ferry had not put to sea, but had moved from one berth to another while in harbour.

Before Zeebrugge it was common for ferries to do that, and I accept that the danger is negligible; but after Zeebrugge? The mind boggles that the new regulations could be considered of so little gravity that a Master could move his ship an inch with the doors open.

Another small, but significant incident convinced me that the whole question of safety and passenger security on board was not being taken seriously. On a trip to Calais a barman telephoned me and said a woman had been injured on the after deck. A door had come off its hinges and struck the head of a British woman in her early thirties. Luckily she had only sustained a graze, and I treated it. She was lucky it was not more serious, as it was a heavy door and could have fractured her skull.

We lashed the door back on and made it secure. The next job was to make an official report, as is required for any passenger injury. I phoned the bridge, and was told to tell the First Mate, who at that moment was having his meal in the Officers' Mess. He was watching *Sins*, the Joan Collins TV mini-series. The correct procedure was that he should have gone down and seen the woman before we docked, established that she was fully fit and did not wish to be examined by a doctor, and then he should have taken her name and address.

But without looking away from *Sins*, he listened to my report with a sort of bored air, and said, 'Just get her name and address and stick it in the book.'

That was typical. Clearly what happened at Zeebrugge had not made some people any more safety conscious or efficient. It was only a small thing, a sloppy, lazy act. But had not Mr Justice Sheen said that the whole company was 'infected by the disease of sloppiness'?

I believe that was how it all started, with the small things. You neglected those, and people thought, 'Well, he doesn't care, why should I?'

So *that* person neglects something small, then a collection of small things becomes a chain, and suddenly it's a *big* thing, and you have funerals, memorial services and inquiries.

I actually heard several crew saying, 'It can never happen again.' And I could have screamed at the point they were so obviously missing. Perhaps what happened at Zeebrugge could never be repeated. Given the stringent new regulations and the obvious awareness of people about it, it was a million to one chance that any British ferry would ever leave harbour with its bow doors open.

But there are other potential disasters at sea: fire and collision to name just two. If people were slipshod about their work and cavalier about safety another accident of a different type might one day happen.

It used to be said that armies were always preparing to

fight the *last* war. The same seems to apply to accidents. When they have happened, everyone knows how to prevent them. But it is not the actual accident itself that is so important in terms of future prevention, as the attitudes and inefficiency that caused them. For they are symptoms of a disease, the disease as Mr Justice Sheen might say 'of sloppiness'. I was beginning to feel that the calamitous happening on 6 March, and the soul-searching that followed, had only put the disease into remission. The symptoms were still there – who knew when a new crisis of fever would arise?

I realised that I could not go on serving at sea on P & O cross-channel ferries for very much longer. I was no longer totally sure of safety on board, and besides, my own personal state had deteriorated alarmingly. I began to imagine that passengers were looking at me, and that they knew everything that was going on in my mind. Sometimes I had panic attacks and had to go up to my cabin to compose myself before I could face people again. I used to look at drinkers in the bar and suddenly they seemed to possess the faces of those *Sun* day trippers, who had been merrily drinking in the bar when the *Herald* went over.

I saw the faces of people from the *Herald*, then they were gone. Once when the *Pride of Free Enterprise* went into Southampton for repairs to a damaged rudder, a couple of us went ashore for a few pints. Across the crowded bar I saw a man who was the exact double of Brian Eades, the Senior Purser who had died at Zeebrugge. I just stared and stared at him, until I realised that a colleague, David Shrubsole, was shaking me and saying, 'Are you OK?'

I had just gone into another world. When I checked the leave book on the *Pride*, instead of seeing the names of its crew, I saw the names of the dead crew from the *Herald*.

And I was bottling it all up. I still felt I could handle days, but I knew that night work, with its darkness and echoes of Zeebrugge, had now become impossible for me.

There were isolated examples of a corporate lack of tolerance for the *Herald* people. A young man called Vince Calder, whose father had died on the *Herald*, was suffering from strain, and unsuccessfully tried to get leave. I said something to him that I have never said to another crewman before. I told him, 'Go sick.' It was clear the system lacked compassion, and he had a genuine case in my opinion. When the senior officers looked at his sickness record, they wanted to give him what is known as a Master's Warning, which is a very serious reprimand. Luckily, I managed to talk them out of it.

But one of the Masters of the *Pride* said to myself and the Senior Purser, 'These *Herald* people are getting to be a problem. We'll have to stop this.'

I felt the hairs on my neck and legs bristle, and my heart began to pound. I could quite easily have smacked him in the face there and then. That Master had attended a lot of *Herald* crew funerals. So if *he* could take that heartless attitude, what about the rest of them?

Subconsciously I made plans to go, deciding that I would not resign immediately but I would take sick leave. I knew then that if I was not sick already, I was on the verge of it, and that I must seek skilled help.

I was not pulling any stunts or con-tricks. I told Anne of my decision and she backed me. I did not tell my colleagues, and I did not tell Anne, of my waking nightmares.

I was working with a man who was learning the job and I found myself cramming him with knowledge, because I now knew I would not be there to help him the following week.

On what proved to be my last day at sea I had mixed feelings. The sea had given me so much – and taken so much. I went to the Senior Purser and told him I would not be back. We docked at 9 in the evening and I went up to my cabin to empty my locker. I came down the stairs with a profound sense of relief.

I was not sad. I was sure, in fact, that I had made the right decision. My local doctor signed me off work with a sick note confirming that I was suffering from stress and anxiety. Technically I was on sick leave, but in my heart of hearts I knew I would never go back. Home was the sailor, home from the sea.

# 16

## *No, Your Majesty*

When I went back into the interior of the *Herald* it was because I felt I could do no other thing. I was scared, but I controlled my tears. I did not think consciously of bravery or its application to me as an individual, nor have I since. I thought then, and I think now, that I did my duty.

But I do strongly feel, that the crew as a whole acted bravely that night, and that P & O have never, ever recognised that fact.

I never, at any time, lobbied for, or suggested myself for any bravery award whatsoever. But I got them all the same. And when I did I felt I was receiving them on behalf of *all* the crew who behaved with such gallantry that night.

Firstly I received a letter on 19 October 1987 from the Order of St John. It informed me that I had been awarded their Silver Life-Saving Medal. Slightly less than two months later I went up to London, for the investiture ceremony in the Order's Grand Prior Church in Clerkenwell. The medal, which is worn on the right breast suspended from a silk ribbon, was presented to me by Lord Grey of Naunton, the Chancellor of the Order.

Afterwards I felt like any other person who gets an award or wins a prize. I felt proud. But as I told the local paper when they interviewed me, I felt I had received it on behalf of the many people who helped in the rescue and the aftermath, and for those continuing to care for the relatives of the victims.

They reported that, but they also described me as 'Mr Homewood, married with two children ...' Well, not yet.

I did not feel like any kind of hero, but I felt proud and somehow gratified, that at last someone had recognised what we had tried to do that night.

Eleven days after my trip to London, another letter dropped onto my doormat. I looked at it carefully, it had 'from the Prime Minister' on the envelope. I thumbnailed it open. Mr N. L. Wicks, Principal Private Secretary to the Prime Minister, the Rt Hon Margaret Thatcher, was informing me that Her Majesty the Queen had graciously confirmed the Prime Minister's suggestion that I be awarded the Queen's Gallantry Medal.

The letter asked me sternly to keep that information strictly secret until it had been officially announced in the *London Gazette* on the morning of Thursday, 31 December.

I had made the New Year's Honours List, and frankly I was flabbergasted. Three other crew members got the same award: Tom Wilson, Billy Walker and Leigh Cornelius. And Andrew Parker, the passenger who had bravely made himself into a human bridge to help save fellow passengers, received the George Medal, the highest peacetime bravery award.

We were to receive our medals from Her Majesty the Queen herself at an investiture in March at Buckingham Palace. By then I would have left the sea altogether. I had no need to fear any reprisals or hostility from P & O.

So when the Queen asked me precisely why I had left the sea, I told her precisely what I believe.

Actually, I am a patriot. I love my country and I respect the monarchy. I believe it is a stabilising factor in our society, and as individuals I certainly have respect for members of the Royal Family such as the Queen herself, Prince Charles and Princess Anne.

I was unashamedly looking forward to the investiture, less for meeting the Queen and getting the award – although the thought of the ceremony made my pulse race and sweat break out – but more for actually getting a peek inside Buckingham Palace itself. Anne was to accompany me, and my brother Robin was coming along too. I told them to savour the day, to take in all the surroundings and remember them. I doubted that we would ever be going back, and this day would be something we would remember all our lives.

I do not know the layout of the Palace, or where the

various rooms are situated, nor for that matter, what the room the investiture took place in was actually called. But I do remember a quietly impressive place, with people quietly and efficiently going about their business. The ceremony took place in a small hall, its walls lined with portraits of regal-looking gentlemen. There were row upon row of seats for families and other guests, and in a small minstrel's gallery, a group of musicians from the Coldstream Guards played a selection of tunes.

It was the New Year's Honours List investiture, so there were a lot of people to be processed, and the Zeebrugge heroes were to be the last.

An official in a black uniform had us in a line outside the hall, ready for us to file in one by one when our names were called. I recognised the Belgian diver with whom I had worked in the dark and the cold that night, the one who had confirmed to me that my pal Glen Butler was dead. I learned that his name was Lt Guido Couwenbergh, of the Belgian Navy. He and I were getting the same award.

Michael Skippen's widow Lynda was also at the Palace to get Michael's posthumously awarded George Medal in a private audience.

Amid all that splendour, the understandable pride at standing before your Queen and receiving an award, suddenly you were brought back to a cold reality. If good men and women and children had not died, and there had not been a catastrophe and others to rescue from it, you would not be there. That thought sobered me. As my name was called I walked through, as instructed, to another usher waiting inside the hall. Then, again on instructions, I first bowed, then walked forward, stopped at the point where the Queen stood on a raised dais, and turned.

I have seen the Queen a thousand and one times on television. You feel you know her, and yet once you are before her it is very different. She is quite small, but because of the raised platform she was on my level. She wore a simple, emerald green dress, and she looked a very soft and kind sort of person.

Perhaps I should not feel this, or say it, as maybe it goes against all the democratic principles of our time, and I believe very strongly in democracy. But I felt proud, that I, Stephen Homewood, a lad from the proverbial humble background, was now speaking to my Sovereign. And if that sounds as though I am fawning and sycophantic, I am not and it is not meant to be. And all I can say by way of explanation is, see how *you* feel if you ever meet the Queen. They say the most ardent republicans quickly fall under her spell.

I think the conversation that followed will show that as patriotic and pro-Monarchist as I am, I did not let the opportunity to speak frankly slip by.

The Queen took the medal and attached it to my lapel by means of a very simple little hook. She then spoke a little short formal sentence: 'This is the Queen's Gallantry Medal in recognition of your bravery on that night at Zeebrugge.'

She then said to me, warmly, 'And how are you now?'

'Fine, Your Majesty,' I said.

'Are you still at sea?'

'No, Your Majesty,' I replied.

Looking concerned, she enquired, 'Is that because of what happened?'

This was the moment. I had a fraction of a second. The easiest thing would have been to have said, 'Yes, Your Majesty.' What did it matter? The Queen was dealing with probably a hundred people that day. She would ask polite questions, but she could not be expected either to know, or deeply care, about the answers. The idea, I knew instinctively, was to have a normal, polite chit-chat, and then leave, and let someone else get their medal.

And I suppose in a way 'Yes, Your Majesty' would have had some truth in it. In a way I *had* left the sea because of what happened that night at Zeebrugge. It was the experiences of that night which gave me nightmares during the daylight hours; which kept me seeing the faces of the dead on the bodies of the living; and which made me super-keen on maintaining safety at sea.

But I knew also that the final and conclusive reason why I had turned my back on the sea was that I no longer trusted my colleagues or P & O in terms of safety 100 percent.

It had become impossible for me to work at sea because safety regulations were being constantly contravened. Before Zeebrugge – as I have showed – although this laxness had concerned me, it did not make me leave. I suppose then, like everyone else, I had thought 'It can't happen.'

Zeebrugge had made me realise that a serious accident *could*, and probably *would*, if that persistent slipshod attitude to safety was not rectified immediately. And there had seemed no chance of this happening, and so I had left.

Now the Queen of England was asking me why I had left: 'Is it because of what happened?'

I felt I owed it to every dead passenger or crewman who had lost their lives on the *Herald*, and to every future passenger sailing with P & O, to speak the truth. My heart was pounding.

'No, Your Majesty. It is because safety procedures were still not being adhered to by P & O,' I answered. It was out!

She seemed startled and unsure what to say next. She made a small noise that sounded like 'Ooh' which became 'Oh ...' and finally, 'Well, I hope you recover soon, and hope that things are good in the future.' She shook my hand quite firmly, and as the Queen broke our grasp, she seemed to give a small propelling movement forward, a mini-shove, as if to indicate that the brief audience was now over.

I walked to another official, who quickly unhooked my medal, put it in its presentation case, and handed it back to me. I was then led out, back into the corridor by another route, and then silently back into the hall through a different door, to join the guests for the remainder of the ceremony.

When the Queen left the hall, she was preceded by a court usher tapping a ceremonial rod into the floor at each step and escorted by Beefeaters, the Yeomen of the Guard. I noticed that the Coldstream Guards musicians were playing a familiar tune. It was the Elizabethan Serenade by Ronald Byng. A logical choice, for this was the second Elizabethan era and this was the second Queen Elizabeth of England.

For me it had a deeper significance, and added to the already unbearable poignancy of the day. It was the tune I had last heard in the cabin of the *Herald*, just minutes before we set sail on the fateful voyage.

Outside, a reporter asked me about my award. I told him, and the words hold good today, 'This honour is for the people who cannot be here today. I also regard it as being for those who died too; who knows what those people did?'

And who can know? Great acts of gallantry, and no one to see them or record them, and then just the long silence of the grave.

Some of the dead had been honoured, like Michael Skippen. His smartly dressed wife, formal in her hat and suit, posed self-consciously for the press photographers with Michael's posthumous George Medal, a small smile of pride on her face. Her words spoke better of how she really felt that day, 'It is a very proud but very sad day for me. I shall never forget why I am here, alone, in his place. I have lost an awful lot. For Michael can never be replaced.'

He could not. And neither could David Disbury or Glen Butler or any of the others, and not all the medals in the world could ever make me forget that fact, or forget them.

There were to be other pictures, official Buckingham Palace pictures, to be a treasured permanent record for us of that day. I posed proudly in my uniform with my medal, Anne and Robin at my side.

I was then given a card to fill out my name and address so that prints could be sent to me, and I was then charged a tenner! The pictures are not free; for each print you want you must hand over £10. I wanted two, one for me and Anne, one for Robin, so I went into my wallet, there in the courtyard of Buckingham Palace, pulled out £20 and handed it to the official photographer. (Actually, I'll probably want more for the rest of the family . . . so it will be more tenners.)

I confess I was surprised and a little disappointed. It was not so much the money as the feeling that something rather special was being sullied. My thought was that if the Palace can have such a grand and impeccably organised investiture – God knows what they cost – could not they throw in at least *one* official portrait free? (Prints extra, of course!) And could they not trust you to pay when the prints come in, rather than have you hand the money over there and then? After all, our credentials would seem to be impeccable.

The day was not over yet. A red-crested invitation with the inscription 'Dieu et mon Droit' (God and my right) urged our presence at 12-30 p.m. at Lancaster House in St James, London SW1 – the Foreign Office.

There, the invitation stated, the Rt Hon Lynda Chalker, MP, Minister of State for Foreign and Commonwealth Affairs, would welcome us to a reception in honour of the Zeebrugge investiture.

This was to be a family affair for us. As well as Anne and I, there would be Robin and his wife, Cliff and his wife Debbie, who had come over from Canada, and my mother and father, who although separated had united for that day. It had been impossible for them all to come to the Palace, but they could all come to the reception. Cliff and I both wear beards and look very similar. That was to cause some amusing incidents of mistaken identity.

Cliff and Debbie arrived at Lancaster House before Anne and I. Lynda Chalker must have been well-briefed, because as Cliff walked up the receiving line she immediately assumed he was *me*. Well, we do share the same surname after all. She started being extremely complimentary, saying, 'Well done', until Cliff said with a polite cough, 'Actually, I'm his brother.' When I eventually did turn up she showed a sense of humour by greeting me with, 'You're not your brother are you?'

Meanwhile, during the busy reception Admiral of the Fleet, Sir John Fieldhouse, went over to Cliff and started talking animatedly about Zeebrugge. He clearly thought also that Cliff was me! When Cliff pointed out that error for the second time, Sir John went, 'Oh . . .' and drifted off. I never did get to talk to the only Admiral of the

Fleet I am ever likely to chat with over a drink.

For by now I had one, a cold and refreshing gin and tonic, which was just what I needed after the nervous tension of the morning and my outspoken remark to the Queen.

Lynda Skippen spoke to me, saying, 'You're Steve Homewood, aren't you?'

She seemed very composed, and when we talked I said what I could to make her feel Michael's death had not been in vain. I told her, 'Michael died at his post.'

Lynda Chalker made a moving little speech and as I looked around the crowd who listened attentively to the words, I saw Lynda Skippen. The composure had gone. She was weeping.

It should have been the perfect day, but it was about to be ruined. After the reception we were due at a lunch hosted by P & O chairman Sir Jeffrey Sterling at the Grosvenor House Hotel in London's Park Lane.

The invitation said Sir Jeffrey wanted to meet me. Well, I suppose he did meet me, but only just. It was literally a handshake and I was moved on. I honestly think that by this time P & O and its management, Sir Jeffrey included, were so sick and fed up with Zeebrugge and its aftermath, that they wanted to be shot of the whole thing. They did not *want* to speak to us, to hear our stories, or even worse, our recriminations. And I believe they were frightened that anything they said to us might be thrown back at them, leaked to the press, or used in some way to damage them or their company.

The whole party of us, Anne and I, Robin and Cliff and their wives, Mum and Dad, were all going to the lunch. And afterwards in the evening, we were going up West, to see *Phantom of the Opera*, a show everyone wants to see. This was my way of treating the family, as I wanted to say thanks, especially to Anne. She had been so kind and understanding, even though she could not really penetrate the kind of psychological hell through which I was going. This gesture was my way of saying, 'I love you' to her and to all of them. I was learning to say it all openly, but I wanted to make some practical demonstration of it.

But there was the lunch first. It was a grand occasion. The menu was in French: Assiette Fumoise, Rosette de Boeuf Rôtie au Jus de Truffe, Bouquetière de Légume, Pomme en Chambre de Robe, Plateaux de Fromage and Café. Which roughly translated, worked out as smoked fish, roast beef in truffle gravy with vegetables, an apple dish, cheeses and coffee. It was washed down by good wines: a dry white Sancerre, Les Calluettes '86 for the starter, and a superb claret, Mouton Cadet Selection Rothschild 1980, with the beef. Port, brandy and liqueurs followed the coffee.

It was a wonderful meal, so it was not the food or wine that gave me indigestion – it was anger. Anger at Sir Jeffrey Sterling, chairman of P & O. George Medallist Andrew Parker, and Michael's widow Lynda Skippen were at Sir Jeffrey's table when he rose to make a speech. He warmly praised the Belgians for their help and assistance, but as I listened in mounting disbelief, he did not say *one* word during the speech to commend the British passengers or the crew.

In fact, apart from that hurried handshake on the receiving line, I believe he did not even acknowledge our presence in the room. Once again it was as if the people from the *Herald* were invisible, even at an occasion to mark the incident that had thrust them to prominence.

I felt the bile rise, and the taste of the fine wines turn sour in my stomach. The day was ruined for me.

At length Sir Jeffrey sat down and the Belgian Ambassador Mr J. P. van Bellinghen made his speech. To my astonishment *he* praised the crew, saying that had it not been for the crew the loss of life would have been greater. I felt an enormous well of gratitude for this man.

The lunch ended and I went to seek him out to thank him for that small, but oh so important, gesture to us. He could not possibly know what it meant at that moment.

When I found him he was talking to Sir Jeffrey Sterling. I am not a rude man, and I do believe in manners and courtesy. They are right and necessary and they help make the world function. But on this occasion I tossed away my ingrained beliefs and habits and I deliberately interrupted their conversation. Sir Jeffrey looked up startled, as I started to thank the Ambassador for his words of praise.

Promptly the chairman of P & O turned on his heel and walked briskly away from us. Within five minutes, he and the other top management representatives of

P & O had left the room. Sir Jeffrey had 'looked forward to meeting' me. I sincerely hope I never set eyes on him again in my life.

We went off to the theatre, my family and I, but I could not settle. And after *Phantom*, as we were leaving the theatre, by sheer coincidence, I saw Malcolm Shakesby, who took control after the capsize, with a man called R. John (I only know his initial) from the Marine Directorate of the Department of Transport.

I had seen them both at the lunch, and now they told me they were off to the Red Ensign club, a Merchant Navy members-only place. They asked me to join them, and by God I felt like it too. I felt like nothing more than sinking a few drinks to blot out the sour memories of that ruined day, and being with people who understood, who were probably as angry as I was. We would get maudlin drunk together, and talk events over for the thousandth time.

That is what I earnestly wanted before I saw the looks on the faces of my family, of Anne and Robin, of Cliff and my Dad. Verbally, Anne included, they all said, 'Go, it's fine, we don't mind. We'll go home on the train. We don't mind, really.' But their faces told another story. It had been my day and theirs, and they had come up to London to share it with me. They were proud of me, and they could not know then that Sir Jeffrey's innocuous words had cut me to the quick, not so much for what they said but for what they *did not* say.

I knew I could not just walk out on them like that. It

would spoil their day, even though they would rather die than admit it. So we all went home on the train together.

# 17

# *One Survivor Can Still Feel His Wet Socks*

The names reel off now like some peacetime battle standard: Bradford, King's Cross, Zeebrugge, Piper Alpha. All catastrophes, each with a human fatality list that speaks of untold grieving and sorrow. And for those who do not die, but are terribly injured, maimed or disfigured, there is the long and agonising haul back to health.

But there are the other victims too: those who survived without apparent serious injury, but who still wake up screaming in the night with their memories. I was just such a casualty.

At first I tried to deny it, even to myself. I was alive wasn't I, and should not that be enough? Surely the rest was just psychological mumbo-jumbo. All I had to do was 'pull myself together', and I would be fine.

Well, I tried hard and it did not work. I had 'pulled myself together' and gone back to sea on a ship that was the twin of the one that had killed so many. I went back and forth across the Channel, as I had so many times before. I listened to the casual jokes, the unwittingly tormenting remarks; I saw the safety omissions, the old pre-Zeebrugge casualness creeping back, and still I worked.

And yet in the end I could not, simply *could not*, carry on doing that work any more. There was something buried within me which came from that night and it had to come out.

I know now that I was not alone. A senior social worker, Janet Johnson, a member of the Herald Assistance Unit which was set up to help people like me deal with our feelings, told a conference last year (August 1988) of some of her findings.

'One survivor can still feel today his wet socks on his feet,' she said. 'Gentle men became violent; aggressive men became apathetic.' She talked of symptoms such as attacks of panic, palpitations, loss of appetite, nightmares and muscle pains. She spoke of careers being blighted, personalities changed.

Zeebrugge certainly haunted me and it still does, although I must say that with skilled help I believe I have conquered the worst part of it.

I have explained how I bottled up some of the fear and grief. Anne was marvellous, but sometimes it is easier to talk to someone who is not as close to you. Occasionally it is less difficult to open up to a stranger. And that is what happened to me.

Things had become very bad, and I was seeing the

faces of the dead on the bodies of the living. I was seeing the names of the dead written where the names of the living had been put down.

It had become harder and harder, and then finally impossible, for me to work on a ship. I was having the panic attacks of which Janet Johnson spoke. I was irritable and moody, and my appetite was severely diminished. Even as I write, the loss of one stone following Zeebrugge has never been replaced, and I wonder if it ever will.

In the early days after the *Herald* tragedy I had bad nightmares. They all concerned – not surprisingly I suppose – water, always masses of rushing water.

But I suppose the most severe effect of this post-tragedy trauma was on my relationship with my wife, Anne. She is a warm and caring person, but is also quite practical and down to earth. Frankly, I think she got fed up with the constant comings and goings in the days following Zeebrugge; the telephone calls, the visits. But mostly I think she got fed up with me, and no wonder. As I have said, I was bad-tempered and irritable, and I took it out on her. She was the person nearest to me, and so became the easiest available target for the bitterness and anger I felt but did not know how to properly express.

I am ashamed to say I used her as a human punchball, not in the physical sense of course, but she was there absorbing the verbal punches. I would fly off the handle at the simplest thing, and Anne would be the one I would have a go at. I felt that, like everyone else, she did not understand what I had been through.

In turn she got to the stage where she would say, 'Look, it's over, it's done with. You've got to forget it.' And *yes*, even 'Pull yourself together'.

Our relationship deteriorated, and although we never did anything drastic like moving into separate bedrooms or talking of divorce, I know that our marriage was severely at risk. I believe that deep down we both knew we would overcome this, and that things would get better. And in the background, of course, affecting everything we thought, was our lovely son, Simon. It is possible that if Simon had not been there, Anne and I might not have survived the aftermath of Zeebrugge with our marriage intact.

Now I am happy to say that our marriage has come full circle, and we are back at the point we were before Zeebrugge made our married life so painful. I know that I must have been unbearable to live with, and I can only apologise to Anne for being so horrible, and thank her for putting up with me until the nastier ghosts of Zeebrugge had been exorcised from my mind.

A group called the Herald Assistance Unit had been set up to help the disaster survivors, and a very kind lady called Jenny Burgess saw me and tried to help me talk about my feelings.

But it was a letter from the South East Kent Health Authority that really made me sit up and take notice, for it seemed they knew exactly what I was going through. They knew that I had received assistance from the HAU, and that I had been offered the services of a

Royal Navy psychiatrist, Dr Morgan O'Connell, who had helped veterans of the Falklands campaign deal with their nightmares. I had not yet taken up the offer to visit Dr O'Connell and his team at Gosport, and the letter was like a Godsend as it seemed to read my mind:

> 'We are very concerned that . . . following the trauma you have . . . experienced, you may well be suffering in a number of extremely distressing ways and you may be worried that you are not getting better by now.
>
> 'The stress of man-made disasters on the scale of the capsize of the *Herald*, is so great that it causes "symptoms" in almost every survivor, no matter how well they felt and coped with their life beforehand . . . we believe that the survivors . . . and their families are a special group with particular psychological problems.
>
> 'You may, for instance, find either that you cannot bear to think about the disaster at all or that you cannot escape from perpetual images and thoughts and feelings which disturb you during the day, and may appear in nightmares which disturb your sleep.
>
> 'You may have frequent headaches or digestive disorders. You may experience fears you never had before – particularly in relation to ships or the sea or enclosed places. You may find your relationships with your partner, family and friends altered in ways which are hard to understand.
>
> 'You may find yourself feeling unusually irritable

and dejected, and you may even feel guilty that you survived.

'In addition there is grief to be borne, with loss of colleagues whom you may have worked closely with for years, and there is the loss of the ship itself which was both your workplace and at times your home.

'There may well be other things which trouble you. All these reactions are perfectly natural.'

I was astounded that they had described so accurately so many areas that were troubling me.

The letter then explained that the writers represented a mental health team consisting of a consultant psychiatrist, community psychiatric nurses, social workers, and a psychologist, all qualified and experienced in working with people in states of distress. They said they would be prepared to see me alone or with my family, or even in a small group. They worked out of a small house next to the Royal Victoria Hospital, but they even offered to come and see me at home.

I said I would go and see them alone. I knew that the things I had to say I could only say to a stranger, and I could not say them in the presence of someone I loved.

At length I went to the team's office, and was introduced to psychologist Penny Dixon. Jenny Burgess from the HAU had listened to me, and listened well. But Penny Dixon not only listened, she knew how to probe. She sensed there was tremendous anger and bitterness inside me that I was bottling up. It may have overflowed on occasions, and led to one or two angry outbursts, but now she encouraged me to articulate my anger and bitterness. I did.

I was angry, really angry. My voice rose as I told her *exactly* how I felt about that night and afterwards. I vented my fury at losing so many of my good friends through (in my opinion) years of safety negligence, which had led to what should have been an avoidable catastrophe.

I poured out my bitterness over what I believed was P & O's washing its hands of the disaster: the gradual smoothing over of the tragedy, the change of name, the repainting of the ships, and the unspoken but clear wish that the *Herald* survivors disappear and 'go quietly'.

And Penny Dixon let me talk, and the more I talked, the greater the weight that seemed to lift from my shoulders. It was as though this invisible burden I carried was getting lighter.

We talked about my symptoms, the panic attacks, my inability to go to sea as a working officer again. I told her how I felt terrible tension, and how my mind seemed to race out of control, with thoughts of the disaster whizzing round in my head. She helped me to learn how to relax. She told me how, when I was tense, or nervous – like at the inquiry – when the adrenalin starts to flow, and the heart pounds fast the way to ease those symptoms. First I was to imagine I was somewhere else, some calm, favourite place. I remembered soaring over the cool, silent Austrian forests in a ski chair-lift. To me that was the most perfect and peaceful place. No noise, no cars or radios, just the crystal clear pure air, the silence and the beauty. So I would imagine that. Close my eyes and try and transport myself above the Austrian treetops. And it worked. I could *feel* myself becoming less tense.

Penny Dixon also taught me how to physically relax my body. Closing my eyes, starting with one muscle or part of my body, and consciously untensing it until it was limp, then another part, and another, until my whole body was like a rag doll. And again, it worked. I had around twelve sessions with her, and they worked wonders on me. I have used her methods since, and they still work today.

I know that I can never be completely 'over' Zeebrugge, but I no longer have nightmares, and though I do think of the tragedy often, my mind is no longer a raging torrent of thoughts, swirling and crashing around.

It was lucky I saw Penny Dixon and her team when I did, and lucky that the South East Kent Health Authority cared enough to have the unit at all. My brain was unscrambled at last, and for the first time since 6 March I felt mentally stable. The National Union of Seamen had arranged for me to see a psychiatrist from London's famous Harley Street. He interviewed me alone and with Anne, and his report shows *just* how lucky I had been.

Dr Peter Storey saw me on the 12 October 1987 in Dover. I give his report in full. There is a natural reluctance to do this – who of us, after all, would want our mental condition laid out for all to see – but I believe it is important to be frank. If it helps one other survivor of a major tragedy, then it will have been worth it. I believe also it will give professional credence to what I have already laid out in this book.

A copy of the report was sent to Messrs Steggles Palmer, of 2 Bedford Row, London WC1, the solicitors acting for myself and colleagues in our civil action for compensation against P & O. It reads in full:

> 'I interviewed Mr Homewood on 12.10.87. I also saw his wife, and I interviewed them separately and together. I had available photocopies of his original handwritten medical notes dating back to early childhood.
>
> 'These show no evidence of any particular psychological vulnerability, and he appears to have been in robust health on the whole.
>
> 'Mr Homewood was obviously extremely tense when he first came to see me. Although he relaxed a little, his manner throughout the interview continued to betray a state of apprehension and anxiety, he was sweating slightly, and told me that his heart was "pumping – it's the adrenalin I suppose".
>
> '... He has in fact been receiving considerable psychological help from the Assistance Unit, and he has recently begun to see a psychiatrist in Folkestone.
>
> 'His symptoms are mainly of continual tension, a feeling of being "stressed", and continuing apprehensions, especially while on board. He is also at times quite markedly depressed in mood, but mainly as an immediate and understandable reaction to some-

thing sad or distressing related to the disaster.

'There is no evidence of any depressive illness as it is usually diagnosed in psychiatric practice. He is much more apathetic than he used to be, and finds it difficult to settle down and help at home, but this is improving.

'The most striking symptom is one which he had for some weeks in April, when he had a strange sensation that his mind was being read by other people who could know what was in his mind without seeing him or hearing him.

'Luckily, this symptom has passed off, but it is usually only found in people with major mental illness such as schizophrenia, and it indicates to me that at that time Mr Homewood must have been on the verge of a genuine breakdown into illness of a serious type.

'That, however, appears to have passed, and there was no evidence of any such symptom when I interviewed him.

'He has not had much trouble sleeping, but he did lose quite a lot of weight in the early stages, which he has not fully replaced. He had previously been a man who enjoyed active involvement in house maintenance, and so on, but he found it difficult to concentrate on this, and has become relatively apathetic about it, as about other hobbies and interests.

'In the earlier stages he tended to pace about "like a caged tiger" and still tends to some restlessness. He has been troubled very much by his memories of having to help identify dead crew members among the other bodies, and the sight of rows of dead children affected him very deeply. He has recurrent visions of one dead child whose open eyes seemed to be looking into his, and he also remembers with horror the way in which, when he was helping one of the rescue divers, the already dead and almost dead had to be just put aside and ignored.

'These and related thoughts still recur intensely and disturbingly. The apathy and the intrusive memories are, of course, characteristic of the post traumatic stress disorder.

'He has been generally irritable and ill-tempered, but his wife told me that he had kept this under good control and had not put too much pressure on her because of this.

'She was not at all surprised that he had sought further psychiatric help, but she said, as he had, that since going off sick three weeks previously, he had obviously improved a lot and was much more relaxed-seeming.

'For many weeks he had tried to stay at work, believing that it was the right thing to do, but he had found some of his work extremely difficult, and continual apprehensions about safety precautions, escape routes and so on, had troubled him a lot.

'At the time of the disaster he had been dealing with leave applications, and when he went to work after the *Vortigern* on the *Pride of Free Enterprise*, he found himself doing the same task, and suddenly found his mind concerned with the man with whom he had been dealing at the time the ship went down.

'That man had actually died, and Mr Homewood found this coincidence of thoughts and feelings very disturbing. On the *Pride of Free Enterprise* he also found himself horrified by some of the safety practices, and people's attitudes, and this was at the time when the inquiry ... was being held.

'... things such as cancelled life-boat drills, a ship sailing without rudder pinned in place, and so on, made him feel extremely worried and angry. He had been intending to continue in his work at sea, but even slightly rough water he found more than he could cope with, and on one occasion when the ship listed slightly he panicked and bolted out of the door and on to the deck, where it took him 20 or 30 minutes to bring his fears under control.

'Mr Homewood comes from a stable sounding background, he has no previous history to suggest any emotional vulnerability, and he has formed a happy-seeming marriage.

'He is suffering from a severe tension and anxiety state, for which he has sought professional help, and he has improved since going off sick.

'He did show earlier evidence that he might be on the verge of a severe breakdown into major mental illness, but that has passed.

'In summary, Mr Homewood is a man of previously normal, stable temperament, who since the disaster has suffered from severe anxiety and tension state, with features also of the post traumatic stress disorder, and who in fact had transient symptoms suggestive of a major mental illness.

'He has sought professional help and is seeing a psychiatrist. It is difficult to give a confident prognosis in view of the published work on this syndrome, but the severity of his symptoms, is, of course, a bad prognostic sign, although the fact that he has improved since going off sick is on the more optimistic side.

'I think it probable that he will continue to have at least some disturbances for a couple of years, even if he does completely recover in the end.'

Signed: Dr Peter Storey.

I was on the point, Dr Storey felt, of totally cracking up and becoming seriously mentally ill. Thank God that did not happen. Canada had helped, as did Anne's understanding and leaving the sea when I did, besides seeing Jenny Burgess and Penny Dixon.

Perhaps my own 'normality', and desire *not* to be ill helped. I have been damned close to becoming a severely mentally sick person, and I realise that Dr Storey is right; I will have 'disturbances' for a couple of years. But I know that I have beaten the worst of it.

However there was no way I could return to work on cross-channel ferries, and on 26 January 1988, I took a medical at the General Council for British Shipping at 6, Castle Hill Road, Dover, and was declared unfit for sea service by Dr Tim Whittaker. He gave me a letter which I took to P & O, and saw their doctor. I was in precisely *seven* minutes before it was agreed I was to leave the company on medical severance terms. I had been with them 13 years, and my days at sea were finally and irrevocably over.

I asked the company for only three things on leaving. A reference; where all the personal objects I had left on the *Herald* were; and if any pictures existed of the interior that would resolve for me the agonising question of how the body, whose arm dangled into my face during the escape, could have lodged. The last was for my peace of mind. I have not yet had an answer to any of the three requests.

Now only two crew survivors of the *Herald* disaster are still with P & O. People have left for various reasons, several sacked by P & O following the National Union of Seamen's strike against the company, and the crew's refusal to accept new terms.

P & O set up a redeployment unit in March 1988 to help employees who had survived Zeebrugge or were to be made redundant. In the event the seamen's strike meant that there were few redundancies, and the unit folded six months later.

The Townsend Thoresen name had gone, the crew – or virtually all of them – had gone or were going. The *Herald* was on the other side of the planet being ripped apart for scrap.

That awful memory was slowly being erased from the public consciousness. And you could almost hear the collective sigh of relief from P & O.

# 18

## *The Man on the Ladder*

I gave my evidence to the inquests held in Dover Town Hall. It lasted 30 minutes.

I was specifically asked about Glen Butler, whether I had seen him and at what stage, and I told them exactly what had happened. I also tried at one stage to point out that quite a few people in the bar of the *Herald* at the moment of capsize had been the worse for wear through drink.

But the Dover and East Kent coroner, Mr Richard Sturt, did not seem to think it was relevant and hurried me over that. I do not even believe a note was made of what I said in that respect. I can see that it might be distressing for families of some of the dead people to say it, but if alcohol could have been a factor in whether some people lived or died, I think this should have been mentioned. People drink; I do myself. And especially they like a relaxing drink on planes and boats and trains. And no one can logically expect an emergency to occur.

But I cannot rid myself of the feeling that some of the dead would be alive today if they had not been drinking so heavily.

I left the inquests after giving my evidence with the strong feeling that what I had to say was not welcome. Most of the pathologists' reports showed death by drowning or hypothermia, or both. The cause of death on David Disbury was drowning; on Glen Butler, drowning and hypothermia; on Clayton Dyer, drowning and hypothermia.

During the inquests, once again the whole tragedy of the *Herald*, the catalogue of faults and mismanagement, culminating in the open doors, had been raked over.

As the evidence of the real-life horror inside that ferry on the night of 6 March unfolded, none summed up more the desperate choices we had to make than the incident of 'the man on the ladder'.

An Army corporal, Peter Williamson, gave evidence that one man was clinging to a rescue ladder for some ten minutes, apparently dazed or semi-conscious and unable to move. But he was blocking the way for other people in the water who were dying. Corporal Williamson told the inquest that he shouted at the man to move, but there was no response. Then he shouted for others to knock the man off the ladder. The man was then shaken off the ladder, fell into the water and was never seen again. A stark decision, to shake him off and let those with the will and conscious ability to live to have a chance.

Mr Sturt said the jury needed at least 'to glance in the direction of murder'. But having had them glance, he then detailed the evidence and directed against any such verdict. The Coroner's officer, PC Bill Maddocks, had made more enquiries after Corporal Williamson's 'surprise' evidence, and it was clear that many other people were shouting for the man to be knocked off the ladder and that no blame attached to the soldier concerned. It was not, the Coroner declared, the action of one particular person and the evidence was far too speculative to think of unlawful killing in respect of murder. Mr Sturt added that even if there had been any such evidence, when killing was a reasonable act of 'self preservation' (which in his judgement included people in great fear and danger of their lives), such a killing was not murder at all.

There is a French phrase 'sauve qui peut', which I believe translates as 'save himself who can' . . . or more familiar to us, 'every man for himself'.

In fact, on the *Herald of Free Enterprise*, it had not been every man (or woman) for themselves in the sense of it being a mad scramble with the weakest going to the wall. As I have recorded, there were many selfless acts of heroism and self-sacrifice from crew and passengers alike. But it was certainly 'save himself who can'.

The man on the ladder clearly could not, and what was worse, he was stopping others from saving themselves. He was shaken from the ladder, and died so that others might live.

In his summing up Mr Sturt told the jury to put aside

their personal feelings against Townsend Thoresen and any thoughts they the jury might have that the company should be 'made to pay for the disaster'.

Neither was the jury concerned with civil or criminal liability on the part of any named person. He recalled that when he began the hearing on 7 September 1987, he had warned the jury that they would hear some of the most harrowing tales ever heard in a British court, and that it would be an immensely complicated inquest.

He told the jury, 'I wonder if any coroner's jury has ever faced a bigger task than you have now?'

The inquests had lasted over four and a half weeks, and eventually the jury took nine hours to bring in their verdicts. But when they did it was a sensation.

In the case of 188 of the *Herald* dead, the jury returned verdicts that each of them had been 'unlawfully killed'.

Many people had expected a verdict of 'misadventure', meaning that it had been an accident, an unfortunate and tragic Act of God.

Because the verdict was 'unlawful killing', there was the direct legal implication that someone was allegedly responsible for the deaths. Legal experts speculated on the possibility that Master Captain David Lewry, First Officer Leslie Sabel, and Assistant Bosun Mark Stanley could even face criminal charges as a result of the verdicts, but at the time of writing no such charges have been brought.

After the inquests, solicitor Mr Michael Napier, speaking for the 120 solicitors representing families of the victims, said, 'The families are pleased the jury repaid the faith shown in them.'

The so-called 'top people's' solicitor, Sir David Napley, who once successfully defended former Liberal leader Jeremy Thorpe at the Old Bailey, also had something to say. Sir David had represented some families and he told reporters it was 'tragic' that Townsend Thoresen had escaped any blame. I say 'Hear Hear' to Sir David.

A report in *The Times* of 13 September by their transport correspondent Rodney Cowton, claimed that ferries were *still* sailing with their bow doors open, less than seven months after the *Herald* tragedy. This had been disclosed by the Department of Transport, who refused to name the ferries concerned. Cowton said reports of *five* such incidents were being investigated.

Dr Jim Cowley, Surveyor General in the marine directorate of the Department, said, 'Recently the Department has received a number of reports of ferries crossing harbours with vehicle doors, bow or stern, open. This is not a safe practice.'

And still P & O's disastrous handling of the whole aftermath continued.

Survivors learned that the three weeks of leave that they had been told to take after Zeebrugge, was to be docked from their annual leave. One ferry crewman had four weeks leave deducted, for the time he had taken off to look after his mother, who had been widowed in the tragedy. Likewise this happened to one father working for the company; his son was one of the crew who died, and the lad's father took the time off to mourn. It was docked from his leave.

In December 1987 a small wood dedicated to the dead of the *Herald* was planted on a one and a half acre site off the A2 at Whitfield in Kent. The trees had been planted by the Kent branch of an organisation called the Men of the Trees, along with students from Hadlow College of Agriculture. P & O bought the site on behalf of the Men of the Trees, from farmer John Dunford. It is to be made up of alder, white poplar, quickthorn, ash, oak, beech, cherry, field maple, guelder rose and dogwood.

The first tree was planted in a morning ceremony, by Mr Peter Ford, chairman of P & O European Ferries. Sir Frederick Bolton, chairman of Dover Harbour Board, planted another. Ford's was an oak, Bolton's an ash. Mr Mike Chaston, Personnel Director of P & O, dug in a field maple.

I know every detail because I read it in my local newspaper. I was not invited, and to my knowledge neither were any other of the crew survivors. Glossing over the hurt I felt, I believed it would be a good focal point, and a place to visit where I could spend some moments in quiet contemplation when thoughts of Zeebrugge became overwhelming.

The site was a secure place, with a locked gate, and relatives had each been given a key. I wrote to the Men of the Trees, whose patron is the Prince of Wales, and asked them if I could have a key to 'Herald Wood' as it was called. Their chairman, a Mrs P.D. Stevens, replied,

'... Unfortunately, the keys were restricted to next of kin only. We do feel however, that any of your friends' relatives would probably be more than willing to loan you a key should you wish to visit the site. We are sorry that we cannot be of more help in this matter. Sincerely.'

I wonder how much a key costs to make, and how many people would demand them? But that passion for the rules shone through. I had seen two of my closest friends, and scores of my crewmates, die on that ship. But I was not 'next of kin'. So I had not been invited to the planting, and I was not to get a key. And Mrs Stevens felt that if I did wish to 'visit' the site, I could just pop round to one of my bereaved friends and borrow one. I do not feel kindly disposed towards the Men of the Trees, an organisation that I had never heard of before nor since.

Perhaps I have weighed my criticisms of P & O too heavily. Let me recount an incident where they *did* try to help. I got a letter from them, a similar letter which went out, I understand, not only to surviving crew members, but also to the widows or widowers or bereaved parents of those who had not survived.

The letter, which arrived about seven months after Zeebrugge, said that the company wished to offer a free holiday to us. That was a generous act, for perhaps a holiday away from it all could help put the memory of the *Herald* tragedy behind us. Where was this get-away-from-it-all holiday? On the *Canberra*, P & O's luxury cruise liner!

There was a choice of cruises, spreading over the whole 12 month period from about September 1987 to September 1988. Anne and I talked about it, and thought, 'Why not?' I had been back across the Channel a couple of times, and I did not want to feel I could never get on a ship again.

The *Canberra*, after all, was not a cross-channel ferry, and most importantly it did not have bow and stern doors. We agreed to go, and left at the end of September 1988.

I was a *little* uneasy about it, but we went anyway. I had wondered a little when the invitation arrived from P & O if it was some kind of trap on the lines of 'Ah, the fellow says he's not fit to work at sea but he can take a trip on the *Canberra*', and especially as the invitation stated that one must have a doctor's letter saying one was fit to travel.

I consulted the lawyers acting for us on the compensation claim, and they assured me it did not prejudice my claim. The cruises were offered on a first come, first served basis, and ours took Anne and I on our first choice, to Malaga, Spain; Aghios Nikolaos, Crete; Port Said, Egypt; Haifa, Israel; and Gibraltar. I'm pleased to say we had a good time, although I feel as critical as ever of P & O's ferry services.

Glen Butler's widow also took one of the cruises, a port of call on that trip for *Canberra* being Las Palmas. The ship docked and next morning she came on deck to see moored next to the *Canberra* . . . the towed wreck of the *Herald of Free Enterprise* on its way to Taiwan for scrapping!

Did anyone, *no one*, know that the *Herald* – renamed *Flushing Range* – would be in Tenerife at that time? And if one person, either on the *Canberra* or at P & O headquarters did know, could someone not have broken the news beforehand to Glen's widow, without her having to wake up and have it hit her in the face like that?

Lyndsy Butler had her two little boys with her, so perhaps the shock had even more impact. But she is a redoubtable woman, and when the initial shock wore off, I think she was glad to have one last contact with her brave husband.

Quite the most appalling and distressing gaffe occurred on the first anniversary of the *Herald* capsize. And it showed either colossal ignorance on behalf of P & O, or a blundering misleading of the public which upset every surviving *Herald* crew member who was present that day.

On 6 March 1988, there was to be a memorial service for the Dedication of the Herald Memorial Window by the Bishop of Dover, the Rt Revd Richard Third, at the Parish Church of St Mary the Virgin in Dover.

The window in question was a beautiful stained-glass affair depicting the plight of the *Herald* that night, the rescue and afterwards. Once again I was not invited. Stewardess Gail Cook, who had been on the *Herald*, also learned of this, and that other crew members had not been asked either. She kicked up a fuss, and my invitation duly arrived. Other C Watch survivors and members of the team who had gone over to Zeebrugge and done such sterling work afterwards, did not manage to get invitations, despite Gail's efforts.

Inside the church that morning we saw a brass plaque inscribed with the names of those who had died. The window itself was in fact two windows, separated by a stone column, the glass stretching high into a rounded nave. These windows were examples of exquisite workmanship. In coloured glass there was the figure of Christ calming the angry waves with the words 'Peace, be Still', while a grieving widow and children kneel before a tombstone engraved 'I am the Resurrection and the Life'. A group of mourners with heads bowed, represent the rescuers and others who gave succour: a sailor, a diver, a fireman, a doctor, a nurse and a helicopter pilot.

The inscription reads, 'In Memory of All Those who Died in the *Herald of Free Enterprise* on the night of Friday 6th March, 1987, off the Port of Zeebrugge.'

Above that was the stained-glass representation of a ship. I say 'a' ship, rather than 'the' ship, because the ship WAS NOT the *Herald of Free Enterprise*! This ship had a completely different superstructure, its funnel was much further to the rear, and painted in white. It was, in fact, the *Pride of Dover*.

Here was a presumably expensive stained-glass window constructed to commemorate the loss of the *Herald*; a permanent monument that, just as we see other stained-glass windows from centuries before, would be seen by generations for centuries to come. And into it had been worked a representation, *not* of the ship that had been sunk, but of a newer and more modern ship.

It was as if for something similar representing the loss of the *Titanic* they had put in another White Star liner.

When I saw it my jaw dropped in disbelief. It could not be, surely? I felt anger in my throat and tears prick my eyes in humiliation.

The *Herald* was in Taiwan now, being converted into pots and pans, or whatever they do with the scrapped remains of what were great ships. Was her memory to be scrapped too? In Soviet Russia they used to rewrite the text books to eliminate the names of Party heroes who had fallen from favour. Would future generations look at this window and think back to a sea tragedy, while all the time looking at the wrong ship?

Not if we could help it they would not.

But how had it happened? Whoever drew or designed the window must have approached P & O for a photograph or artist's impression of the ship, and maybe even a detailed plan of her.

How then, if he had been given the correct picture or drawing could he have got it wrong? He could not. And if he had not approached P & O and had simply worked off newspaper library pictures or snapshots, he surely could not have been given the *Pride of Dover* by mistake.

But let me suggest that it was all some terrible mistake. The rest of the crew who saw it were as angry as I was, and we resolved to do something about it. We approached the church authorities and pointed out this appalling blunder. They were as upset as we were and promised they would have it changed.

And I am delighted to say they did. The window now contains a picture of that lovely, tragic ship the *Herald*, with the distinctive blue funnel with its TT logo in white.

In case anyone doubts the mistake was made, I have kept the proof. Two colour postcards. Both were taken by a photographer called Ray Warner, and printed by Noel Tatt Ltd, of Coombe Valley Road, Dover. The first clearly shows the two windows, with the *Pride of Dover* where the *Herald* should be on the left-hand window. On the reverse of the picture handed out that day is the list of services for Holy Week of 1988. The second shows the *same* section of window with the *Herald* in place of the *Pride*. On its reverse the information states that it is a limited edition postcard, and there is space to write a name, address and brief message.

There are, it seems, only 1,000 copies of that picture available. I certainly hope that the *original*, and shall we say erroneous, postcard is no longer available.

That day, dismayed and unsettled by what had occurred, the crew members left the church after the service and went down to the seafront at Dover. There on a miniature jetty we threw an anchor-shaped wreath into the sea. The air was cold and the water grey, just as it had been a year before.

But there was to be yet another snub. The Belgians held a service to open a memorial to the *Herald* dead in Zeebrugge. I was not invited, nor as far as I am aware, were the other crew survivors. Tom Wilson and John Jackson happened to be on duty on the Zeebrugge run that day, and so they went. Only one paper, to my knowledge, highlighted the hurtful ignoring of us. That was the Communist daily, the *Morning Star*, who made it their splash story with banner headlines.

A medal had been struck by P & O and handed out that day. It consisted of a large silver circle, and on one side there was a map showing the areas of Dover and Zeebrugge with the Channel between them, and on the reverse the points of the compass. On the blue box the inscription reads, 'This commemorative medal was struck by P & O in appreciation of the unique assistance rendered at Zeebrugge on the night of March 6th, 1987.'

And yes, I finally received mine. It arrived unheralded and unaccompanied by any note of explanation. Someone came round and pushed the medal in its box through my letterbox. The first warning I had of this glowing tribute from P & O – who had not thought fit to invite me to the original ceremony – was a distinctly unceremonious clunk as it landed on my hall floor. My only thought is that P & O must have minted a lot and, having some over, had them delivered to us as an afterthought.

There were more storm clouds on the horizon. Members of the National Union of Seamen working for P & O went on strike over new working arrangements.

The NUS claimed that these new working arrangements, which covered manning, would mean a reduction in the number of crew on duty and would be dangerous.

I agreed and told the local newspaper at the time, 'Cutting down on staff is madness. I believe there is bound to be another ferry disaster some time. It could be for a number of reasons – perhaps just because a crewman was overworked and overtired.

'With the amount of pressure the long working week will put on crew members, safety will suffer. They are cutting crews and cutting wages. Ferries have to sail in bad weather conditions because the only thing that is important to the management is making money. People simply cannot be as efficient when they are tired. The new plans will be a giant step backwards. I would not work the hours they are asking, and I am glad I don't have to.'

For their part P & O claimed that they would not do anything to jeopardise the standards of safety they had achieved. They stated also that the number of crewmen on the ships at any one time would not be reduced, and that there would not be undue pressure on crews.

The strike led to bitter scenes on the picket lines, as some people either carried on working or returned to work defeated, as the strike dragged on.

I happen to believe that in this case the men were striking in everyone's best interests: this means the interests of the passenger. The men did not wish to see safety further jeopardised.

P & O eventually responded by sacking those who refused to return to work and sign the new working agreements. The strike and P & O's arrogant obstinacy left a legacy of bitterness in the town of Dover and the villages around, where seafaring dominates life.

The *Herald* in 1987, the strike in 1988. Heroes one year, sacked strikers the next. The bitter memories will not heal in a lifetime.

# 19

# *The Ghosts Are Fading*

I am not religious, and I did not pray or ask God for help on that night, or since. I have no disrespect for religion, and I found some of the services and the hymns extremely comforting.

Yet although I do not agree with orthodox religious views of God, or Heaven or Hell, I am no longer frightened of death.

I have witnessed violent and sudden death at close quarters, and my best friends have been among those claimed. I have seen the newly-dead at close quarters, and I have gazed into 'the windows of their souls'.

And I truly believe the dead are at peace. Death is clearly not welcome, except in the case of extreme age or pain, but when it does come, as it inevitably does to us all, it is not something which should induce terror.

Zeebrugge has made me feel, and I regret that I cannot put my feelings into a better framework of explanatory words, that the dead are truly at peace, removed from the torments of life and in a kind of natural harmony. I do not expect this to be a comfort to those whose friends and loved ones died on the *Herald*. None of us wish to see those dearest to us snatched away so suddenly.

But if there is any consolation, the people I saw at that makeshift mortuary in Zeebrugge, whatever their final moments had been like were, at least and at last, at peace.

Having seen that, as well as just how quickly and violently life can end, has altered how I feel about my own life. I was very reserved; I felt unable to express love, unable to tell the people closest to me just how much I cared for and treasured them. It seems very un-English, and somehow unmanly, to say to your father 'I love you' and hug him. There seem to be confines on who we can express our love to. A wife, yes, a child, yes, but not a dear friend, male or female, a brother or a father.

Now I no longer have such inhibitions. And no longer do I think in terms of tomorrow or next week, next year. I am not concerned with pensions, or retirement plans.

I am not suggesting that provision for the future is unwise – clearly it is *very* wise – but I am more interested in NOW, this moment, this minute, this day.

How is the infinitely precious commodity of life to be spent? How is it not to be wasted? I have learned to recognise the beauty of the world around me; I was in too much of a hurry to notice this properly before. Yes, birds singing (how sweet they sounded on that morning I returned to my home from Zeebrugge), the smell of grass and flowers, the beautiful colours of my garden. I marvel at the beauty of my wife, and the untold riches of having a dear son to hold in my arms.

Materially I am not wealthy. I am OK: I have a house, a car, a new job. But all those material things we think are so important, I have learned are not.

The really important thing is the way we live our lives, how much we give out, and the way we receive the love that others offer to us.

I am also very concerned about the way we treat the planet on which we live. Someone once coined the term, Spaceship Earth and it is so apt. There *is* nowhere else for us to go. And we have seen just how much pollution, the cutting down of the rain forests, the extermination of species, is hurting the world.

I have a son, and I want him to grow up and enjoy a fruitful, bountiful world with its natural wonders intact. Not a chemically despoiled world, where the fish can no longer swim in the sea, and the birds can no longer sing.

The night of 6 March 1987 has made me aware, as I was not before, that our surroundings are beautiful, and that we should help keep them so.

No, I do not sit cross-legged in my house in Folkestone, contemplating a flower with a serene smile on my face all day. I am still a normal man leading a normal life. And I still get depressed and angry occasionally, and I am no saint to say the least. But despite that, all I have just said holds true for me.

Life is richer and sweeter, and the joy of being alive is counterpointed only by the knowledge of those so dear to me who are no longer here, and who cannot enjoy the things so many of us take for granted.

It could so easily have been me in that water, unconscious from a blow on the head and drowning, or drifting away from life slowly, my body gripped by hypothermia.

But I survived and because I am alive, I have a duty to LIVE. And because of the circumstances, I have a duty to speak out as honestly and forthrightly as I can, when I believe that others could die from the disease which erupted so violently at Zeebrugge. I have been asked whether I am obsessed with the *Herald* tragedy, and in one sense this is almost an insult. In the clinical 'sick' sense of obsessed, no, I am not. But in the sense of being fascinated, enthralled, unable-to-forget-what-happened sense, yes, I confess to that obsession.

Occasionally when I have made a strong statement of anger or bitterness in this book, I have asked rhetorically, 'Wouldn't you be?' Well I ask it again, 'Wouldn't you be obsessed?' Just a little? Wouldn't you, if only at intervals, turn over in your mind the events of that dreadful night? Wouldn't you wonder if you could have done more, and think, like I do, 'If only I'd gone into the water for Glen when I said I was going to?' If only ... I believe you would have just as many of them as I have.

But there are sides to the disaster which could lead to help for future victims. I believe firmly that there exists now the professional talent to put together a pool of help ready to be called on in the event of another disaster. I do not mean for rescues, they seem to be ably coped with by the services on the spot, but rather in the aftermath. A team of dedicated doctors, nurses, social workers, psychologists and psychiatrists trained in post-disaster trauma treatment.

If that mass of experience, which must exist now following the major disasters we have had, with its reams of data and information, could be concentrated into one unit, I believe it could be invaluable in the future. I hope that some government agency or voluntary body is bright enough and far-sighted enough to organise such a Disaster Aftermath Unit.

I will never forget that night, *never*. As I said in the introduction, this book has been a form of exorcism for me. Somehow, talking it out, putting it down, examining my feelings on paper, has been good for me.

I feel strongly too that there should be something on the record by someone who was there, saying how it REALLY was. I have now written out the worst of the ghosts, the worst of the nightmares, and the blackest of the memories.

But there remain some ghosts that will never leave me, and nor would I wish them to. For to banish them would be to forget what they remind me of. They are ghosts of memories. The memory of Glen, floating in his lifejacket. The memory of that last conversation with David Disbury. It is important that I keep those, for they prove how lucky and privileged I am to be alive.

Do I feel a hero? No.

I feel I am an ordinary man, but one who took his job and his duty seriously. When the *Herald* went over there was no question in my mind that I would do my duty. I suppose I might have died. But I know one other thing; that I could not have lived with myself if I had not tried to rescue as many passengers as I did.

I believe the British seaman is second to none in the world, and that when it comes to that crunch he will do his duty unto death. I went to enough funerals to know that proved true on the night of 6 March 1987.

There have been harsh words for P & O in this book, and I retract nor apologise for them. But this book was not meant to be a bitter diatribe against P & O. It is meant, both as a record of Zeebrugge and its aftermath, and as a tribute to the brave of that night.

This book has been *my* story, my personal account and my recollections. But it is also their story. The story of the brave people who lived – and the brave people who died. The book is for them.

I shall never forget them. *We* should never forget them.

## CREW OF THE *HERALD OF FREE ENTERPRISE* ON 6 MARCH 1987

*Barry Allen, *second cook*
Terry Ayling, *bosun*
*Dick Barnard, *assistant quartermaster*
Martin Barnes, *steward*
*Lee Birtles, *catering storekeeper*
*Gerry Brazil, *cook*
Keith Brown, *fourth engineer*
*Lynda Burt, *stewardess*
*Daniel Burthe, *steward*
Clive Bush, *steward*
Tony Bushby, *steward*
*Glen Butler, *steward*
John Butler, *steward*
*Percy Calder, *steward*
Gail Cook, *stewardess*
Paul Cormack, *steward*
Leigh Cornelius, *seaman 1A*
*Robert Crone, *chief engineer*
Richard Curner, *assistant cook*
*Stan Darby, *chief petty officer motorman*
Nick Delo, *crew messman*
*David Disbury, *assistant purser*
Tony Down, *seaman 1A*
*Clayton Dyer, *steward*
*Brian Eades, *purser*
*Graham Evans, *electrical officer*
*Steven Ewell, *steward*
*Terry Frame, *senior barman*
*Nick Gough, *steward*
Henry Graham, *kiosk steward*
Steve Greenaway, *seaman 1A*
*Geoffrey Haney, *cook*
Dave Hawken, *senior duty free shop steward*
*Dean Hayward, *motorman*
*Barry Head, *steward*
*Steve Helkvist, *cook*
*John Hobbs, *seaman 1A*
Ken Hollingsbee, *steward*
Stephen Homewood, *assistant purser*
John Hudson, *senior barman*
John Jackson, *steward*
Brian Kendall, *seaman 1A*
*Ian Lawson, *steward*
Jenny Leslie, *stewardess*
David Lewry, *master*
*Angus Mackay, *second cook*
*Robert Mantle, *radio officer*
David Matthews, *foreign exchange cashier*
*Alan Medhurst, *steward*
Graham Merricks, *steward*
*Ivor Moat, *cook*
Mick Mordue, *third engineer*
Danny Morgan-John, *steward*
Paul Morter, *second officer*
Phil Naisbitt, *quartermaster*
*Ted Oldfield, *steward*
Max Potterton, *deck storekeeper*
*Edge Quested, *steward*
Nick Ray, *second engineer*
*Marie Richards, *stewardess*
*John Rodgers, *motorman*
Les Sabel, *chief officer*
*Dave Santer, *steward*
*Mick Skippen, *head waiter*
Charlie Smith, *assistant purser*
*Tony Spink, *steward*
*Stephen Sprules, *junior catering rating*
Mark Squire, *seaman 1A*
Mark Stanley, *assistant bosun*
Mick Stickler, *steward*
Moyna Thompson, *senior stewardess*
*Christopher Thumwood, *second engineer*
David Tracey, *steward*
Mick Tracy, *carpenter*
Billy Walker, *seaman 1A*
*John Warwick, *steward*
Paul White, *chief cook*
Tom Wilson, *quartermaster*
*Kevin Worsley-Smith, *steward*
Daniel Wyman, *junior catering rating*

*Dead

## ABOUT THE AUTHORS

Stephen Homewood was the Assistant Purser on the *Herald of Free Enterprise*. In January 1988 he left P & O, and now works for a hotel in Folkestone.

Stuart White is a Fleet Street journalist. His third novel is to be published later this year.

*The acclaimed bestseller now in paperback!*

# NO TIME TO WAVE GOODBYE

True Stories of Britain's 3,500,000 Evacuees

BEN WICKS

With an introduction by one-time evacuee MICHAEL CAINE

'By this time I wanted my Mummy and Daddy and to go back in that little terraced house all together again. Later, in a strange cold bed at the end of that long weary day, I hid under the bedclothes and cried. Then I remembered that we hadn't said our prayers and with this as an excuse I climbed into my brother's bed while he said, "Gentle Jesus..." At the end of our prayers we curled up together and my little five-year-old brother said, "Don't cry, Jean, I'll look after you."'

'Ben Wicks, himself an evacuee, has compiled a moving and fascinating book' – Mary Wesley, *Daily Telegraph*

'Absorbing and frequently touching' – Philip Oakes, *Listener*

'Unique... Mr Wicks has caught all the pathos and the humour of those traumatic times in a moving book' – Derek Naylor, *Yorkshire Evening Post*

You saw *Tumbledown* on TV – now read Robert Lawrence's own story…

**When the Fighting is Over**

# TUMBLEDOWN

***A Personal Story***

JOHN LAWRENCE and ROBERT LAWRENCE MC

'A blunt, sometimes shocking account of how a cruelly hurt young man grappled with a world which no longer seemed to care for the victims of war, once the fighting was done… read this disturbing book' – Michael Toner, *Sunday Express*

'An indictment of petty bureaucracy and military insensitivity. It is also the tale of one man's courage' – *Observer*

'Hardened as I am by a lifetime's reading as a professional military historian, I cannot remember anything more shocking…' – John Keegan, *Sunday Telegraph*

0 7475 0288 9   £3.99